A Pig Don't Get Fatter the More You Weigh It

D0558549

Classroom Assessments That Work

Phyllis Jones,
Judy F. Carr, *and*
Rosemarie L. Ataya, *Editors*

Teachers College, Columbia University
New York and London

Published by Teachers College Press, 1234 Amsterdam Avenue, New York, NY 10027

Library of Congress Cataloging-in-Publication Data

A pig don't get fatter the more you weigh it : classroom assessments that work / Phyllis Jones, Judy F. Carr, and Rosemarie L. Ataya, editors.
   p. cm.
 Includes bibliographical references and index.
  ISBN-13: 978-0-8077-4754-4 (pbk : alk. paper)
  ISBN-13: 978-0-8077-4755-1 (cloth : alk. paper)
  1. Educational tests and measurements. I. Jones, Phyllis. II. Carr, Judy F. III. Ataya, Rosemarie L.
 LB3051.P574 2007
 372.12'6--dc22   2006028930

ISBN-13: 978-0-8077-4754-4 (paper)
ISBN-13: 978-0-8077-4755-1 (cloth)

Printed on acid-free paper
Manufactured in the United States of America

14 13 12 11 10 09 08 07   8 7 6 5 4 3 2 1

# Contents

Part Three:
Organizing and Using Assessment Data

 # Acknowledgments

Together, the editors and their coauthors are grateful for the encouragement and recognition of this project provided by Dr. Laurey Stryker and Dr. Peter French at the University of South Florida Sarasota–Manatee. It was the skilled facilitation of Dr. Janice Fauske that led to the conception and development of the idea for this book during a faculty retreat.

Thank you to Brian Ellerbeck at Teachers College Press for his continued support and counsel. Also, we would like to acknowledge the contribution of Bill Stapleton and Julia White for their eye for detail and Julia's final editing. We appreciate suggestions offered by Doug Harris of the Center for Curriculum Renewal regarding the technical aspects of assessment. And, most important, we extend our deepest gratitude to teachers, administrators, and students in the Manatee County, Sarasota County, and DeSoto County School Districts in Florida with whom we have had the good fortune to work and learn together.

Introduction

Phyllis Jones, Judy F. Carr, and Rosemarie L. Ataya

"A pig don't get fatter the more you weigh it" is an English proverb that refers to the farmers of old and their practice of continuing to weigh their livestock for indications of profit. In this continual weighing, the farmer was distracted from the feeding, which had an ultimate negative impact on the well-being and final weight of the animals. Weighing the livestock was an important part of the farmer's responsibilities, but not to the extent that it distracted from other crucial elements of farming practice. Similarly, in an era of high-stakes accountability, it is essential to balance periodic large-scale state assessments with rigorous, responsive, and ongoing high-quality assessments in the classroom in order to create a vibrant and comprehensive portrait of student performance. Learning and teaching are nourished by continuous feedback using multiple measures and modes of assessment.

This book is intended primarily for practicing teachers and administrators who promote and use assessment as a vehicle for instructional improvement. It is a useful guide, too, for preservice students preparing to teach and lead in schools. The book provides a practitioner-friendly, research-based approach and uses a format and language that engage the reader with a variety of assessment issues from an authentic school and classroom perspective.

The book is organized into three parts. The two chapters in Part One introduce contemporary issues related to assessment in the classroom. Here the authors present systems of support for classroom assessment within the school, district, state, and federal contexts. The process of assessment for teaching that integrates curriculum expectations and individual learning needs is offered as a valuable method that will help the classroom teacher to create classrooms that facilitate inclusive practice. Specifically, strategies are discussed related to the focus, quality, and impact of assessment in classrooms and schools.

Chapter 1, Classroom Assessments That Work, presents considerations to help teachers and administrators clarify the context for classroom assessment, choose the right types of assessments for identified purposes, and establish quality control by setting criteria for high-quality classroom assessments. Chapter 2, Inclusive Classroom Assessment, discusses the guiding principles of inclusion and the role of assessment in teaching students who have diverse learning needs.

The three chapters in Part Two present practical uses for assessment that are appropriate for diverse student populations. Moreover, we discuss how achievement data from assessments provide educators with valuable diagnostic information to improve classroom practices and student learning. These chapters help educators forecast and manage student achievement.

Chapter 3, Performance Assessment in the Elementary Grades, provides suggestions and examples for ways in which embedded classroom assessments can be aligned to desired learning expectations and to effective current teaching practices. Chapter 4, "Can You Listen Faster?" Assessment of Students Who Are Culturally and Linguistically Diverse Learners, highlights the need to understand the influence of students' culture and language on learning, to relate students' achievement orientation to instruction and assessment, and to include students' continuing motivation in assessment. Chapter 5, Using Informal Assessments to Monitor and Support Literacy Progress, shares approaches to literacy assessment that help teachers look at individual children.

Part Three explores assessment practices such as organizing assessment data and using data to inform practice. In the four chapters in this section the authors offer examples of teachers' organizing within schools to create a collaborative response to assessment results that creates a school culture of support for teachers and student learning. Additionally, the potential of action research to inform teachers about student learning is explored. Last, this section turns its attention to how parents can be involved in the assessment process so they may further enhance teaching and learning.

Chapter 6, Policy and Technical Considerations for Classroom Assessment, provides an overview of legislation currently affecting education, describes types of assessment that teachers can use to evaluate teaching, and discusses the technical considerations of various assessment procedures. Chapter 7, Action Research and Classroom Assessment, explores a five-part process of using action research to improve classroom assessment: identifying problems of practice, focusing inquiry questions, collecting data, discussing and interpreting data, and taking action and changing one's practice. Chapter 8, Collaboration to Strengthen Classroom Assessment, focuses on teachers' coalescing around systematic data collection and interpretation for continual improvement of instruction in relation to student needs. Chapter 9, Involving Parents in Classroom Assessment, analyzes some of the reasons why we would want to involve parents in classroom assessments; provides practical ways in which teachers can do this; and explores potential questions a parent may have regarding the assessment policies and practices in school, along with possible responses that a teacher may give to such questions.

Throughout, the book includes examples and tools that the reader may use when creating, selecting, or adapting assessments for the classroom. Vignettes and examples are presented throughout the book, and except where otherwise noted in the chapters themselves, these are composite representations drawn from the diverse experiences of the authors across multiple schools. Also, except in the few cases in which individuals mentioned in chapters are linked to specific schools or organizations by name, the teachers and administrators named in the book have been created by the authors for the purpose of exemplification.

The chapters of this book were written by faculty members from the four separate departments—Childhood Education, Measurement and Research, Educational Leadership and Policy Studies, and Special Education—that constitute the College of Education at the University of South Florida Sarasota-Manatee. The idea for this book emerged unexpectedly during a retreat where we discovered shared values regarding classroom assessment set against a background of our diverse philosophies, experiences, and areas of expertise. From these have emerged the multiple dimensions of classroom assessment presented in this book.

PART ONE

Contemporary Issues in Classroom Assessment

In this section, the nature of contemporary classroom assessment is discussed. This discussion constructs the context for subsequent sections of the book. The multiple dimensions of classroom assessment are highlighted as schools respond proactively to an evolving climate of assessment: a climate in which school administrators, school leaders, and teachers respond positively to the accountability issues of high-stakes testing, as well as to the various forms of assessment that can inform teaching and learning. The diverse nature of students in school, and the creation of inclusive assessment processes, form a discrete focus of this section. Diversity is defined in a holistic way to encompass the many different groups of learners a teacher will encounter in the classroom. Through this, the importance of differentiated and sensitive assessment processes that create a continuous relationship to instruction is discussed. To be able to create such differentiated and sensitive assessments, a teacher must possess a strong knowledge base of different types of assessment processes and strategies, as well as an ability to understand the different learning profiles of an individual student or groups of students. This knowledge base also allows teachers, school leaders, and administrators to make professional judgments in relation to the adoption of whole-class and whole-school systems of classroom assessment.

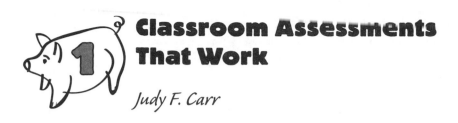

Classroom Assessments That Work

Judy F. Carr

Chris Costello, the principal of a metropolitan middle school, is determined to deepen the focus on effective assessment across classrooms in her school. She has noticed some of her teachers making promising shifts from overreliance on selected-response (multiple choice, true-false, matching) and short-answer tests to constructed-response assessments of products and performances. Nevertheless, she is concerned that new rubrics and checklists focus too much on the products themselves (e.g., the number of pages in the report, how neat the paper was) rather than on expectations for learning (e.g., using the research paper to assess expository writing). Believing that multiple and meaningful assessments of learning are critical, Ms. Costello initiates a process of having teachers identify those areas in which students are doing well on the state assessments, generate hypotheses about why they are, and brainstorm ways that the teachers will integrate those approaches as a regular part of the life of the school. Through this process, teachers develop a checklist of criteria for high-quality assessments in the classroom, and faculty meeting time each month is then devoted to working in small groups to critique and discuss teacher-made assessments and samples of student work. Frustrations with state assessments fade into the background as teachers' collective efforts to redesign their own assessments reenergize the faculty.

Principals, teacher leaders, and teachers are faced with many challenges and dilemmas while shepherding effective assessment processes in classrooms and schools. Apparent conflicts between state and classroom assessments, norm–referenced and standards–based tests, or performance assessment and multiple choice scoring can be resolved through the design of schoolwide assessment systems that employ multiple measures, quantitative and qualitative data, and informal and formal approaches to providing regular and appropriate feedback to learners, parents, teachers, and policy makers.

Implementation of high–quality assessment in classrooms and schools involves creating a balance of rich assessment information about the strengths and needs of students, the curriculum, and the school through a continuous process of vision, exploration, inquiry, and dialogue (Carr & Harris, 2001).

Teachers are helped to expand the dimensions of their classroom assessment practices by engaging in the following considerations:

1. Clarifying the context for classroom assessment, including the levels at which assessments are used for decision making;
2. Choosing the right type of assessment appropriate for use in the classroom; and
3. Establishing quality control by setting criteria for high-quality classroom assessments.

CONSIDERATION ONE: CLARIFYING THE CONTEXT FOR CLASSROOM ASSESSMENT[1]

Classroom assessment fits within a larger context of data gathering for multiple purposes (McMillan, 2001): to improve student learning, to provide data for instructional improvement, to provide data for school and district improvement, and to respond to state-level accountability needs (Sheinker & Redfield, 2001). The assessments in the system complement one another by providing related information at different levels of precision gathered at various points in each student's schooling. By using each appropriately and by examining the results across measures when making decisions, the teacher, the school, and the district have multiple tools with which to monitor the system's impact, instructional effectiveness, and the students' learning (Vermont Department of Education and Vermont Institute for Science, Mathematics, and Technology, 2002).

The Vermont Department of Education and the Vermont Institute for Science, Mathematics, and Technology's *Leadership Advisory #1: Technical Considerations at Four Levels: Tools and Resources for Local Comprehensive Assessment Systems* (2002), from which much of the material below on the four levels of assessment is abstracted, defines a school's multidimensional comprehensive assessment system as including individual assessments, classroom assessments, school/district assessments, and state assessments. Indeed, state assessments, school/district assessments, and classroom assessments could be used together to make decisions about individual student performance in relation to standards (e.g., whether a student is or isn't meeting certain mathematics standards), to make decisions about modifying classroom instruction for all students (e.g., whether more instructional focus is needed on mathematics problem-solving skills), and to make decisions about the focus of school improvement (e.g., whether professional development is needed in the area of mathematics content knowledge). Decisions made through classroom assessment fit into the context of assessments at four levels.

Level One: Decisions About Individual Students

Assessment is first and foremost a matter of focusing on individual learners (Stiggins, 1997), allowing them opportunities to self-assess; offering them feedback about their learning; and diagnosing and responding to their interests, strengths, and needs. In addition, it entails, where appropriate, providing modifications and alternative assessments for students with identified different learning needs and informing placement in courses and programs, as well as decisions about promotion and retention. More important, learners need opportunities to self-assess and to identify their own individual learning goals in order to personalize their own learning process.

Level Two: Classroom Decisions

Classroom-level assessments provide information that is useful in day-to-day instructional planning and delivery. All students need to have the opportunity to be taught and assessed in the classroom before encountering any particular knowledge or skills on a high-stakes test (Popham, 2003). Classroom assessments can range from formal to informal. Students need multiple opportunities to receive feedback about their learning in relation to standards and curriculum objectives for their grade level. Assessments used need to meet technical standards that are appropriate for classroom assessments (see Chapter 6). And finally, individual student learning styles need to be taken into consideration in creating or selecting classroom assessments.

Quality control can be assured through several means:

- Opportunities for teachers to share and critique their classroom assessments, using agreed-upon criteria.
- Opportunities for ongoing, high-quality professional development about technical aspects of assessment and effective assessment practices, including managing the classroom assessment process.
- Access to a database of valid, reliable classroom assessments.
- Opportunities to engage in collegial conversations about peer review of classroom assessments.

- The use of district/school and state assessments for a portion
  of the standards to serve school improvement and accountability
  needs as well as to provide a cross-check with classroom
  assessments.

The primary purposes of assessment contributing to classroom decisions are to improve instruction, to monitor how well students are progressing throughout the year toward attainment of standards, and to improve student learning.

Level Three: School and District Decisions

Schools and districts have the opportunity to design assessment systems that incorporate and expand on the state assessment system and that
serve as a sort of system of checks and balances for classroom assessments.
The primary purposes of school and district assessments are:

- Setting school and district improvement goals;
- Documenting the progress of cohort groups from year to year;
- Action planning;
- Strategic planning;
- Guiding curriculum development and revision;
- Determining staffing needs; and
- Public reporting/local accountability.

The school/district assessment system provides a richer profile of student and school performance than can reasonably be achieved through
state assessments alone and helps to document the following:

- How well students in the district have achieved standards;
- How well the school/district has carried out laws, policies, and
  procedures that support student achievement;
- How well qualified teachers are to teach the standards, including
  certifications and other training;
- How effectively the school has maximized students' opportunity
  to learn by keeping them in school;
- How the school has created a safe and effective learning environment; and
- How well schools have used the resources they have been given to
  maximize students' opportunities to learn.

Level Four: State System Decisions

State accountability systems are systems for reporting selected pieces of data about student learning and the factors that affect or influence student learning for purposes of determining the success of the educational system. The system is used as a means of holding schools and their supports accountable for how well students are learning. Typically states are accountable for

- Demonstrating the impact of and results from laws and funding passed by the legislature and Congress, such as No Child Left Behind (see Chapter 6) and the Individuals with Disabilities Education Act (see Chapter 2) and
- Demonstrating the impact and results from policies and procedures of the department on how well students have mastered standards and how well schools have functioned.

Used at the state level, state assessments serve a primary purpose of accountability, improving school performance, guiding policy for improving schools, and guiding research and evaluation.

                                    ❧   ☙

Understanding the varying purposes of individual student, classroom, school/district, and state assessments can help educators to move beyond "either-or" notions of assessment to build a truly comprehensive assessment system within the school and district. Within such systems, classroom assessment plays the most crucial role in providing ongoing, regular feedback to students about their learning.

CONSIDERATION TWO:
CHOOSING THE RIGHT TYPE OF CLASSROOM ASSESSMENT

Classroom assessment requires a variety of assessment tools that are selected for their appropriateness for the students and for assessing the identified learning, depending on whether this learning involves knowledge, skills, or dispositions. Within the two overarching categories of assessment, which are selected-response assessment and constructed-response assessment, there are four types of classroom assessments, as follows:

- Selected response;
- Constructed response—short answer;

- Constructed response—products; and
- Constructed response—performances. (McTighe & Ferrera, 1996; Vermont Department of Education and Vermont Institute for Science, Mathematics, and Technology, 2002)

Selected-response assessment includes examples such as multiple choice, true-false tests, and matching items. Students are asked to select from answers to provide the correct response. An answer key is the scoring guide used to determine each student's performance, and the score usually becomes the numerical grade. The scores are highly reliable, provided the tests are valid—that is, that they test what they purport to test. These conventional, objective tests are commonly used to quickly assess knowledge of particular content and facts. Essential issues to consider when constructing a selected-response test are the following (Oswego City School District, n.d.):

- What is the primary purpose of the test?
- What knowledge and thinking skills will it assess?
- How much will each question on the test be weighted?
- Is there only one correct answer for each question?
- Have students had the opportunity to learn the information being tested?
- Will the test be engaging for students?
- Will the test be challenging, yet not frustrating?

After a selected-response test is given to students, it can be valuable to analyze any issues that might be evident about the test itself. For example:

- Did the test adequately test what had been taught?
- Were there any flaws in the wording of test items?
- Did students demonstrate any misconceptions about the concepts being tested?
- Is there a need to reteach?

Constructed-response—short answer assessments require that students generate a response by filling in the blank with a single word or a short phrase, or students may be asked to label a diagram or map. They may be asked to show their work or the steps they went through to get an answer. The response is not provided to them to choose, but instead they must create their own (Oswego City School District, n.d.).

Constructed-response—products assessments are artifacts that remain when the work of students is done. They are created by students, and they include such items as written narratives, science lab reports, multimedia presentations, posters, maps, and graphs.

Constructed-response—performance assessments involve students in doing something, and they are an excellent way to assess student learning of processes and skills. Performances are assessed through systematic observation by teachers, peers, or others, using an observation survey, a checklist, or a task-specific or generalizable rubric that includes criteria focused on the desired learning outcomes.

Adopting a schoolwide template for developing classroom assessment plans can support teachers as they work to balance the use of all four types of assessments in their classrooms (Carr & Harris, 2001; Glatthorn, Carr, & Harris, 1996). Teachers in several school districts that worked with the Center for Curriculum Renewal used templates such as the one shown in Figure 1.1 to identify the desired learning for students taken from their local standards and core curriculum, the student work assessed, and the scoring guide to be used. Essentially, the "student work" column provides a way for teachers to identify the *what* of the assessment—whether the assessment is selected response or constructed response, the name of the materials used, and so forth. "Scoring guides" shows the *how* of assessment, that is, the basis for feedback that is given, such as a checklist, an answer key, a rubric, or a teacher observation survey. This is a way of organizing assessment information that helps to directly align the assessment with the desired learning. An example is shown in Figure 1.2. As teachers within a school use a template such as this one, they develop a common language for assessments and a shared structure for selecting, creating, and sharing classroom assessments.

FIGURE 1.1. Assessment Plan Template

Standards (Core Curriculum)	Student Work	Scoring Guides

FIGURE 1.2. Sample Assessment Plan

Standards (Core Curriculum)	Student Work	Scoring Guides
Students observe the way one form of energy can be transformed into another form of energy present in common situations (e.g., mechanical to heat energy, mechanical to electrical energy, chemical to heat energy).	Think-a-loud (Constructed Response—Performance)	Teacher Observation Survey (TOS)
Energy and matter interact through forces that result in changes in motion.	Quiz (Selected Response—Multiple Choice and Constructed Response—Short Answer)	Answer Key
Students describe how forces can operate across distances.	Ball Toss Project Demonstrations (Constructed Response—Performance)	Task-Specific Rubric for the Ball Toss Project
Ask questions to clarify topics, directions, and/or classroom routines.	(Constructed Response—Performance)	Teacher Observation Survey (TOS) for the Ball Toss Project
Compare and contrast information on one topic from two different sources.	Ball Toss Project Report (Constructed Response—Product)	Report Rubric (Generalizable Rubric)
Know and correctly spell level appropriate high-frequency words.	Ball Toss Project Report (Constructed Response—Product)	Report Rubric (Generalizable Rubric)

CONSIDERATION THREE: QUALITY CONTROL

Finally, school leaders can support successful classroom assessment by working with teachers to develop clear criteria for high-quality assessments. Once, when the author was conducting a workshop on assessment for elementary teachers using material from Judith Herman (1996), a 1st-grade teacher raised her hand and asked, "Can you put all these points you're talking about on one sheet of paper so I can laminate it to check every assessment I use in my classroom?" This led to a simple checklist of key assessment concepts that teachers can use for their own assessments or to conduct peer critique of teacher-created assessments (Glatthorn, Carr,

& Harris, 1996). The original checklist has been through several iterations as educators in schools in several states have revised it to best meet their own needs, as shown in Figure 1.3.

FIGURE 1.3. Classroom Assessment Checklist

Congruent

- Assesses the targeted standards, key ideas, competencies, and /or performance indicators.
- Assessment type (constructed response—short answer, product, or performance) is appropriate for assessing the identified content, skills, or dispositions.
- Provides exemplars of student work in relation to standards, key ideas, competencies, and/or performance indicators.

Systematic

- Uses multiple measures.
- Uses appropriate criteria and procedures for scoring and reporting results.
- Shows alignment with the scope and sequence and with classroom instruction.

Ongoing

- Regularly provides feedback to students about their learning in relation to standards, key ideas, competencies, and/or performance indicators.

Inclusive

- Enables all students to show their strengths and show what they know and can do in a variety of ways (e.g. writing, speaking, interacting, and visual representation).
- Involves students in self-assessment.
- Permits appropriate accommodations/modifications.

Technically Sound

- Is valid.
  - The standards, key ideas, competencies, and/or performance indicators that are taught are being assessed.
  - The assessment assesses what it purports to assess.
- Is reliable.
  - The assessment provides sufficient information to make dependable decisions.
  - The results are likely to be consistent from student to student and over time.
  - Has clear language.

Ethical

- Is fair.
- Avoids bias.

Note. Used with permission of the Center for Curriculum Renewal, informed by work with the Enlarged City School District of Middletown in New York; the Franklin Northeast Supervisory Union in Vermont; the Oswego City School District in New York; and the Washington Central School District in Vermont (see *www.curriculumrenewal.com*).

Using this checklist or a variation of it, classroom teachers can analyze their own existing assessments to determine strengths and needed revisions. When teachers in grade-level groups or interdisciplinary teams use the checklist, they develop a common language to guide their discourse about assessment.

IMPLICATIONS FOR SUPPORTING
SUCCESSFUL CLASSROOM ASSESSMENT

Not long ago, a teacher in the final session of an in-service course on classroom assessment shared with her classmates a rubric she had created. As the peer review process went along, the teacher, using a checklist similar to the one in Figure 1.3, was clearly surprised to discover that the assessment actually did not assess the learning she had identified as being the focus of her lesson. Concerned about her need to finish the in-service course, she raised her hand and asked the instructor, "Does this mean I have to change the assessment?" and then clapped her hand over her mouth as she realized the import of her question.

Because many teachers never had a course in tests and measurements as part of their teacher preparation program (Stiggins, 1997), they value structures and supports for improving their own classroom assessment practice. This includes a conceptual framework for understanding the larger context into which classroom assessment fits, an overview of the four types of assessment from which they may select, and shared criteria for high-quality classroom assessments. With tools such as these at their disposal, school leaders such as Chris Costello, the principal in the vignette at the beginning of this chapter, can help to open a dialogue about assessment among classroom teachers and provide the opportunity for them to improve their practice and, thus, to enhance the experience and the learning of the students they teach.

NOTE

1. The material in this first section of the chapter is abstracted with permission from the Vermont Department of Education and the Vermont Institute for Science, Mathematics, and Technology's (2002) *Leadership Advisory #1: Technical Considerations at Four Levels: Tools and Resources for Local Comprehensive Assessment Systems.*

Inclusive Classroom Assessment

Phyllis Jones and Susan Sheffield

It is 4:00 P.M. and mentor teacher Miss Adams tells the interns she is going to demonstrate to them the need for differentiated assessment in a differentiated classroom. She tells them that they will do a hypothetical exercise that demonstrates her points about differentiation. She hands out graph paper to each of her interns and says she wants them to draw "X's" in each box. She then demonstrates an appropriate-quality "X." She instructs them to complete as many "X's" in the squares as they can in the next 60 seconds. After a minute she asks people to call out how many "X's" they successfully completed. Numbers from 2 to 38 are called out (with laughs and sighs), which Miss Adams writes on a continuum line on her board.

She turns to the interns and poses the question, "Say that this week I am teaching 'X' making to you. Do I do the same thing with those of you who correctly made 2 'X's' and those of you who managed 38 'X's'?" She then goes on to share her observations about how the interns approached the task. For example, the intern who only completed 2 "X's" filled all the boxes with one diagonal line but only managed to complete 2 whole "X's" at the end of the 60 seconds. Miss Adams also talks to the interns about how, were she to really teach "X" making, she would assess her students' understanding and application of when and how they would use "X's." She would do all this before she began to think about planning her unit of work on "X" making.

Working in a differentiated classroom demands that a teacher's instructional-strategy repertoire be extensive, creative, and flexible. Indeed, there are many guides and activity books that support teachers in developing this range (e.g., Hammeken, 2000; O'Moore, 1997; Tilton, 2000). This level of importance reaches new heights when we think about an inclusive classroom that welcomes and celebrates diversity. Diversity is a broad-ranging concept that can be seen to encompass students who, because of gender, ethnic background, socioeconomic status, differing ability levels, distinct learning styles, or disabilities, may have academic needs that require varied instructional strategies to help them learn (Hamerstrom et al., 2002).

In a classroom that welcomes learners with diverse strengths and needs, assessment must support teacher decision making in relation to the differentiated instruction, which has natural implications for assessment practices. The nature and form of assessment in any school is complex; such complexity becomes greater when considering assessment practices in an inclusive classroom of students with diverse learning needs. Students may learn a particular skill in different ways and at varying rates; teachers assess student knowledge and levels of skill through student performance. This can be accomplished through standardized and performance-based assessments. Sometimes a teacher has choice over the format of assessment and sometimes this choice is restricted (e.g., state-mandated standardized tests). When there is a choice, a teacher must decide which form of assessment best matches a particular skill base and a student's learning profile to ultimately record performance and progress and to inform future instructional practice. In this chapter we discuss the guiding principles of inclusion and the role of assessment for teaching, a process that offers insight into what teachers may teach; how they may teach; and, ultimately, how well they teach.

THE MOVE TOWARD
GREATER INCLUSIVE PRACTICE

In the 2004 reauthorization of the Individuals with Disabilities Act (IDEA), Congress clearly spelled out the right of all children to a free and appropriate public education (FAPE). It supports the idea that a child should be educated with peers in the regular classroom, unless the four elements of FAPE cannot be guaranteed. These four elements mandate an education that

- Is at public expense, under public supervision and direction;
- Meets standards set by the state educational agency;
- Includes appropriate placement in the state school system (preschool, elementary, middle, and high); and
- Is provided in conformity with the student's Individualized Education Plan (IEP).

Through IDEA runs the concept of a least restrictive environment (LRE). According to this policy, school districts are required to educate students with disabilities in regular classrooms with their nondisabled peers, in the school they would attend if not disabled, to the maximum extent appropriate. Different states, schools, and, indeed, classrooms interpret the notion of LRE in many different ways. However, the policy demands that both general education classrooms and special education services engage in attitudinal and systemic change for enabling students with diverse learning needs to receive a free and appropriate education there. Tilton (2000) describes the inclusive classroom:

> A sense of community pervades the inclusive classroom. This sense of belonging goes beyond the classroom walls to parents and resources in the community itself. Together, adults and children form a partnership of respect for individual differences and a willingness to work together to help all students learn. (p. 16)

Advocates of inclusive education claim "One size does not fit all," suggesting the need to change and adapt teaching and learning in classrooms to meet the needs of a changing and diverse population of learners.

As we become more cognizant of the need to offer different teaching and learning strategies to students who learn differently, we also need to become better at the way we choose and use assessment processes and strategies in the classroom (Gregory & Chapman, 2002). This shift in awareness of individual differences among learners requires that we embrace the notion of difference in assessments that take into account the modifications and accommodations afforded to learners in classrooms. However, before we move on to this, it is essential to recognize and appreciate the multiprofessional nature of ongoing assessment for students with identified disabilities. Multiprofessional input may come through individual student need, arising from the IEP, or system and organizational demands, such as alternate assessment procedures. Potentially, this may mean that a number of professionals are involved. At a simple level, this can be general and special education teachers collaborating together. At a more complex level, this can mean the participation by other professionals, such as speech, language, and occupational therapists; behavior specialists; and child study, transdisciplinary, and other school and district teams set up to support instruction and assessment for students with disabilities. A classroom teacher is the central professional working with the student in the inclusive classroom. He or she must make sense of such multiprofessional perspectives and integrate them into meaningful instruction.

THE ROLE OF ASSESSMENT

The research literature describes a direct relationship between assessing student performance and subsequent teaching strategies (Airasian, 2000; Mindes, Ireton, & Mardell-Czudnowski, 1996; Phye, 1997). Assessment forms an integral part of the teacher's classroom dialogue, particularly in the process of informed decision-making, and how the choices a teacher makes in relation to assessment in the classroom are a reflection of the "teacher knowledge of the subject, students, assessment principles, instructional practices, and the relationship with the student" (Brookhart, 1997, p. 165). Classroom assessment theory places the students in the center of classroom assessment processes that welcome varied assessment strategies (Brookhart, 1997). Brookhart believes that assessment is at the heart of motivating all students to make the appropriate effort to achieve to the best of their ability. Her philosophy offers this chapter a clear and simple way to explore key dimensions of assessment for teaching in the inclusive classroom from the perspective of knowledge of the subject, knowledge of the student, assessment principles, instructional practices, and relationship with the student.

Knowledge of the Subject

A teacher must have a sufficient level of subject knowledge that becomes the foundation of any assessment and teaching. Despite the furor surrounding statewide, high-stakes tests, some teachers are using the assessment results to improve their instructional practices (Gagnon & McLaughlin, 2004). What is important is that these changes are of benefit to diverse learners. In the vignette at the start of this chapter, Miss Adams clearly has knowledge of "X" making and feels it is important to carry out a pretest of that knowledge base among her students before she begins to plan her teaching. Preassessment of subject knowledge becomes an increasingly important element of an inclusive classroom where students bring varied levels of knowledge about the subject to be learned. Gregory and Chapman (2002) have outlined the purposes of preassessment as an information-gathering exercise designed to determine:

- The student's existing level of knowledge about the subject to be taught;
- The standards, objectives, concepts, and skills the student already understands that relate to the subject knowledge to be taught;

- The additional instructional and mastery opportunities that may be needed;
- The subject knowledge that may need reteaching or enhancement;
- The student's areas of interest and attitudes toward the subject; and
- The optimum group structure for the teaching of the subject knowledge.

It is essential that teachers be cognizant of both curriculum and existing student knowledge in order to successfully differentiate instruction in the classroom, but the process of assessment to inform teaching is not the responsibility of one person. A collaborative approach to classroom assessment combines the subject expertise and pedagogical experience of a group of professionals with the abilities and needs of the students. School administrators and classroom teachers are challenged to make this process manageable and worthwhile and have at their disposal a variety of curriculum-based measurements to assist them in assessing students' knowledge and abilities at the beginning of instruction, as well as tracking knowledge acquired as the result of instruction.

Running records (see Figure 2.1) provide one method of assessing knowledge and skills before, during, and after instruction.

FIGURE 2.1. Running Record Template

Grade Level Reading Expectations	Name of Student:		
	Date	*Progress*	*Comment*
Predicts ideas or events in text			
Makes inferences and generalizations about text			
Selects appropriate meaning for a wording based upon context			
Summarizes text			
Progress Key	√ Success without adult prompt > Success with adult prompt X Continue instruction		

Knowledge of the Student

In classrooms that celebrate diversity, students are allowed to learn differently, and as demonstrated in the vignette at the beginning of this chapter, students bring varied levels of knowledge and experience to the learning. The different ways that students learn must influence the assessment practices employed in classrooms. Tomlinson (2001) considers the student differences relating to "experience, readiness, interest, intelligences, language, culture, gender, and mode of learning" (p. 24) and suggests that these elements need to play an integral role in classroom assessment processes. They offer the teacher a way to develop a student profile that offers a potential bridge into teaching the subject knowledge. For children with an IEP, this is a point where information from the IEP is integrated into curriculum planning and, as a result, the teacher makes accommodations (Gagnon & McLaughlin, 2004). A synthesis of studies promoting the development of greater inclusive practice in assessment and teaching, which identify student profiles as a central assessment tool, collectively advise developing student profiles (Castagnera, Fisher, Rodifer, & Sax, 1998; Hammeken, 2000; O'Moore, 1997). Such a profile may include sections that help educators understand their students on many levels such as those illustrated in Figure 2.2.

FIGURE 2.2. Sample Student Profile

Section One	Student strengths and interests (i.e., interest in sports, music, fine arts, etc.)
Section Two	Preferred teaching and learning strategies (i.e., visual, auditory, kinesthetic)
Section Three	Individual Education Plan (IEP) and/or Academic Improvement Plan (AIP) goals and objectives
Section Four	Communication/language strategies
Section Five	Behavior strategies
Section Six	Health and medical issues
Section Seven	Family issues
Section Eight	The contribution of students and families to assessment, planning, and teaching

The teacher may have access to numerous assessment strategies relating to academic performance, but in developing a comprehensive student profile, it is important to recognize the aspects of development outlined above. Increasingly, educators are encountering more assessment strategies related to multiple intelligences that respond to strengths and preferences in learning. Valuable insight can be gained by assessing the areas of multiple intelligences identified by Gardner (2000). Naturally, when one is assessing multiple intelligences, the traditional approaches to assessment need to be expanded to include other forms of assessment such as the Teele Inventory for Multiple Intelligences (Teele, 1997) or the Multiple Intelligences Survey (McKenzie, 1999). Campbell, Campbell, and Dickinson (1999) offer a manageable approach to assessing dimensions of multiple intelligences through interviews, surveys, and observation of varied tasks and also offer practical strategies about translating the subsequent assessments into effective teaching and learning. They approach the intelligences through a developmental model that helps to move the student from a novice to an inventor in each dimension. In addition, they stress appreciating the different intelligence domains when planning and delivering teaching and learning. This becomes crucial when considering a class of diverse learners who may struggle in academic performance assessment but demonstrate strength in one or more domains of multiple intelligences. The vignette of Miss Adams's "X"-making lesson illustrates this idea. She began with a diagnostic assessment to determine whether her students knew how to make "X's." She learned that several students were not proficient at "X" making and designed a lesson to teach the skill. As her lesson progresses, Miss Adams is cognizant of her students' learning styles and modifies her instruction and assessment practices to reflect this. She carries out short probes periodically to determine whether the students are indeed mastering "X" making. Examples of how Miss Adams does this are as follows:

- *Verbal/linguistic dimension:* Miss Adams explains "X" making to the students and assesses their understanding verbally.
- *Logical/mathematical dimension:* Miss Adams demonstrates an "X"-making pattern, such as drawing diagonals in one direction and completing the "X's" by drawing the diagonals in the opposite direction. She encourages the students to develop their own patterns to assess their "X"-making mastery and assesses their final product.
- *Bodily/kinesthetic dimension:* Miss Adams has her students practice

and demonstrate their ability to make "X's" by drawing them on the chalkboard, whiteboard, or overhead projector.

- *Visual/spatial dimension:* Miss Adams shows her students pictures where "X's" are hidden, and she supports their visual search strategies and assesses how many they are able to find and identify.
- *Musical/rhythmic dimension:* Here Miss Adams plays a particular piece of music each time they practice "X" making and when she assesses them.
- *Interpersonal dimension:* Miss Adams allows students to work with partners or in small groups to practice "X" making, but she collects individual information on each of her students.
- *Intrapersonal dimension:* Miss Adams encourages her students to reflect on their ability to make "X's" and mediates their appreciation of what they need to work on to improve. She ultimately assesses their "X"-making performance.
- *Naturalistic dimension:* Miss Adams structures a treasure hunt for "X's" around school and takes students on a short walk to discover "X's" in the environment. She assesses how many "X's" each student is able to find and their search strategies.

From this it becomes clear that although Miss Adams sets up different instructional strategies to accord with different learning preferences, she is able to assess her students' "X" making based on their performance in each of these dimensions. From the examples above, for some dimensions the assessment is similar and for others it is slightly different. Miss Adams collates her assessment information in a student profile. Such student profiles will differ in depth and nature between students depending upon their strengths and areas of need.

Assessment Principles

The way a teacher employs assessment processes and strategies in the inclusive classroom have a major impact on the success of the inclusive practices. The need for assessment to inform instructional practices is central to this argument. The relationship between a teacher's philosophical approach to assessment and subsequent classroom assessment practices is strong. Indeed, the principles a teacher holds about the purposes of assessment influence the practice of assessment in the classroom (McMillan & Nash, 2000).

A strong emphasis must be placed on "assessment for teaching" that is an ongoing process integral to the philosophy of the classroom.

Ongoing assessment, such as running records or performance portfolios, is the process of gathering information in the context of everyday class activities to obtain a representative picture of children's abilities and progress (Dodge, Heroman, & Charles 2004). The process and product of ongoing assessment should directly influence planning and teaching. It is important that this attitude about assessment be fostered, particularly in this era of accountability that No Child Left Behind has engendered. When standardized testing is mandated, teachers tend to teach to the content of the test without diversifying their instructional practices; but when performance-based assessments are used, teachers will increasingly integrate assessment with their instructional practices and continuously refine such practices (Trepanier-Street, McNair, & Donegan, 2001). In their study of teachers' views of assessment practices in the classroom, Trepanier-Street et al. (2001) found that teachers felt that assessment should relate to the teaching or curriculum objectives and offer support to plan for individual students. For example, in reading, a teacher will use a standardized test to ascertain a grade-level score for a student; this score could then be used to account for student progress or school placement. However, a performance-based assessment of phonemic strategies will help a teacher plan instruction of reading strategies that reflect student performance at that time.

McNair, Bhargava, Adams, Edgerton, and Kypros (2003) argue for the further use of performance assessments and contend the following:

Teachers learn that classroom assessment can provide ongoing information about student learning and its relationship to the curriculum goals and how assessment actually supports learning while the information is being gathered. The use of performance assessments can positively affect motivation, interest, critical thinking and the acquisition of more in-depth knowledge. (p. 29)

The process of assessment to inform teaching can improve the quality of the learning experience. Assessment should be seen not as an "add-on," but as an integral part of a classroom ethos that supports all learners in fulfilling their potential. This is especially useful when students are included in the process through their being allowed to keep track of their progress toward academic and behavioral goals. Performance portfolios are one way of achieving this goal.

Many educators use performance portfolios as a method for assessing students' progress in an ongoing way. This method of accumulating students' work has many benefits. It results in authentic, curriculum-based assessments created by students in the course of classroom instruction. It takes into account the modifications and accommodations that teachers employ when instructing students with learning differences. Most important, however, it allows students to be intimately involved in the assessment process and thus allows students to track their progress through the goals and objectives designated in their IEPs and Academic Improvement Plans (AIPs).

While this is an assessment tool embedded in practice, a significant amount of time may be required to organize and evaluate the work that teachers and students choose to include in these portfolios. One method for dealing with this difficulty is to designate a file drawer (or a crate, perhaps) for student folders. Students would be responsible for placing completed, graded assignments in their folders. Teachers and students would then choose representative work samples to include in student portfolios.

Assessment and Instructional Practices

The teacher's instructional repertoire must also be accompanied by appropriate and sensitive assessment strategies that celebrate progress and inform future planning. These strategies may not be very different from the repertoire that teachers possess. McNair et al. (2003) reported that the types of assessments used by elementary teachers for formative and summative purposes are paper-and-pencil tests, observation notes, and student portfolios.

Paper-and-pencil tests encompass the whole area of gathering information from students via pen-and-paper activities including teacher-made curriculum-based tests, standardized tests, and textbook-based tests (Trepanier-Street, McNair, & Donegan, 2001). Indeed, this form of assessment, although widely used, excludes a whole group of students who are not able to respond effectively to paper-and-pencil tests. Additionally, these assessments, if standardized, often preclude the use of test-taking accommodations (such as additional time, scribes, or computers) that students have been allowed to use in other test-taking situations.

The second form of assessment, observational notes, is more promising in assessing information about instructional practices. Making regular and ongoing observations of how students respond in the classroom can be a very valuable assessment tool, particularly if these are made using a systematic and defined protocol that bears a direct relationship to the desired student learning (O'Moore, 1997). There are varied formats that observation schedules can take, depending upon the type of data that a teacher wishes to collect about a student. For example, a teacher may wish to gather general information about how a student is responding to specific curricular experiences. Figure 2.3 illustrates how a teacher is able to collect performance information about Austin, who is in the literacy center writing a story about his family as part of a unit he is working on that focuses on families or habitats. Figure 2.4 illustrates how a teacher can use a time-sampling observational format to collect information about a young child in a group context. Here one sees how Devlin is responding to the learning context, including interaction with his peers over a period of time. Through this the teacher will be able to identify emerging patterns, which informs her future instruction with Devlin.

FIGURE 2.3. Sample Observation Sheet

Name of Pupil: Austin Morrow   *Date:* October 20, 2005

Setting: Literacy Center   *Time:* 9:30 A.M.

Observation:
Austin is in the literacy center writing a story about his family as part of a unit he is working on that focuses on families or habitats. He is joined there by two other students (Brianna and Tyler) working on the same project. They rarely interact, as each child is very intently focused on their work. Austin has written the following notes in his journal/notebook: some key words that he plans to use in his story, a list of each member of his family, his home address, the names of two towns where his family has lived, and the name of the town where his father is currently living.

After approximately 20 minutes Austin has written seven sentences describing his family. His writing contains a variety of sentence structures; has good punctuation; and has a beginning, an opening sentence, a middle portion, and a concluding thought as his last sentence. The writing reflects that of at least a 4th or 5th grader and he demonstrates great intensity and focus as he completes the task. The work is carefully done, thorough, and well presented and organized. He almost never spoke to the other children in the literacy center except to ask about the spelling of a word. When given the correct spelling, he immediately continued with his work. He also reread and reviewed his work and made several spelling corrections or changes in punctuation.

FIGURE 2.4. Sample Observation—Time

Time of Observation	Name of Pupil: Devlin
	Date: September 6, 2005 Setting: Prekindergarten
8:45 A.M.	Devlin, Mariah, London, and Vanessa are building a shopping mall in the block area. They began their work at 8:40 and all but Vanessa are using different types of blocks to work on their structure. At 8:55 London states that he needs all the long unit blocks to make the outside walls of the mall. Devlin has finished placing all the second-longest unit blocks and had just begun to use the longest blocks. London insists on using all the longest blocks and tells Devlin he must give him all those blocks. Devlin refuses and promptly hits London on the arm at 8:57.
9:10 A.M.	Devlin is in the library corner looking at the class book that was written last week and placed in the library on Monday. Two other children are in the library corner looking at other books. When Latosha asks Devlin to let her look at the class book, he refuses and holds it close to his chest. Danny pleads Latosha's case to Devlin, but he still refuses to give up the class book. When Latosha tries to take the book away, Devlin hits her on the hand at 9:13.
9:50 A.M.	Devlin is in the housekeeping/dramatic play area where he is pretending to be the father with Kerry and Mariah playing the roles of child and wife. Devlin is ordering Mariah to prepare his breakfast and telling Kerry he must go upstairs and brush his teeth and get ready to go to school. All three are very focused on their roles and seem to be playing intently and cooperatively. There is no disruptive behavior as the three continue to play until 10:15 when the children go to the playground for outside play. No more hitting occurs the remainder of the day.

Another form of observational technique is event sampling. Figure 2.5 illustrates how event sampling can be used to collect data on a student in relation to a particular event. In this example, the teacher is recording information about London's completion of activities in the classroom. However, continual observations can be very time consuming and create a massive amount of data that is difficult to analyze and use. Indeed, teachers need to be taught when and how to carry out observations so that they can make an informed choice about using this strategy in their classroom assessment. Focused observations of specific activities, for example, students' responses to direct instruction or performances during group learning activities, can be very powerful, especially when conducted by more than one adult. The way we can focus observations in the classroom is by setting up an observational schedule beforehand. The schedule should include the behaviors the teacher wants to observe, the questions that the observation is intended to address, and the times and circumstances of the observations (i.e., every morning for a week during the reading class).

FIGURE 2.5. Sample Observation—Event

Time of Observation	Name of Pupil: London Date: September 14, 2005　　　　　Activity: Completing a task
8:20 A.M.	London finishes the calendar activity without being prompted.
8:35 A.M.	London completes the math activity after being reminded once.
9:15 A.M.	London is not able to complete the math practice sheet and says he cannot finish the work.
10:15 A.M.	London completes the literacy activity.
10:30 A.M.	London completes his writing activity.
10:45 A.M.	London finished reading his story.
11:00 A.M.	London completes his science activity.

Finally, student portfolios can offer one of the most effective ways of developing an assessment process that allows differences to be recognized and celebrated. An advantage of a portfolio is that it has the potential of involving the teacher, student, and others in collecting and evaluating student responses and work. The portfolio records student performance. Even though for some students this may not necessarily demonstrate progress, it does offer a concrete record of their current response to learning. This is particularly important for students whose rate of progress is much slower than that of their peers. Gregory and Chapman (2002) set out the purposes of a portfolio: a collection of student work chosen on specific criteria that provides evidence that the student understands a particular skill or concept. Portfolios can be developmental, and through their review, both student and teacher can make decisions about future learning and teaching.

Relationship with the Student

The assessment practices a teacher adopts are in some way a reflection of the quality of the relationship the teacher has with the student (Brookhart, 1997). This becomes highly pertinent in a classroom where students present diverse learning needs. Two possible scenarios illustrate this point. In one, the teacher sees such diverse needs as a challenge to the status quo of his or her classroom. The teacher may see this as a problem. Consequently, the relationship between the teacher and the student may not be entirely positive, and there may be a reluctance to include different assessment and instructional strategies. In another scenario, the teacher welcomes diversity and is likely to change practice continually. The student is seen as a valuable member of the classroom and varied assessment practices are sought to improve teaching and learning. Through the relationships that have developed in the two scenarios, the impetus to change assessment practice is very different.

The importance of teachers' views of the students is reiterated in the work of McMillan and Nash (2000), who indicate how a variety of factors, including benevolent feeling toward students, influence how teachers use assessments to modify their teaching practices reflectively. Research carried out with student teachers has revealed that, prior to working with children with special educational needs, student teachers expressed strong feelings of negativity and fear toward them. However, when these teachers' interaction with the children was mediated in a positive way and they were supported in developing a range of appropriate teaching strategies for this group of learners, their attitudes towards the children improved (Bishop & Jones, 2002). This illustrates the importance of continued professional development. Through such careful professional development experiences, teacher attitudes toward and relationships with students who are different can be explored and enhanced.

MANAGING DIVERSE ASSESSMENT IN THE INCLUSIVE CLASSROOM

Frequently, concerns are raised about how to manage diverse assessment processes in the classroom. Multiple forms of assessments, including tests, observations, and portfolios, create a mass of paper to be managed. Different schools and even classrooms may have different approaches to assessment management systems. The ideal system is manageable, transparent, and consistent. A manageable system calls for the teacher to make decisions about what key pieces of assessment are kept to demonstrate moments of progress or decision making. For example, creating individual student folders that integrate key curriculum and IEP performance evidence can be one effective way of managing a diverse assessment system in the classroom.

It is important that the information that goes into the folder is evaluated from the perspective of value to the teacher and student. For some students the evidence in the IEP part of the folder may be greater than the key curriculum part, which reflects the individual learning needs of the student. Teachers and students can create and follow an evaluative rubric to help make decisions about what is included in such a folder. These folders should be made accessible to students in an appropriate way to ensure that students are aware of what is in the folder and also appreciate their own role in the assessment process. Such folders can be stored as a file folder in a small filing cabinet. The evidence that is kept in the integrated student folders can include student work, teacher-generated assessments, school- and district-generated assessments, and photographs of student work or students at work. At significant times during the school year the teacher can go into the folder and share this evidence of engagement and progress with parents.

IMPLICATIONS FOR CLASSROOM ASSESSMENT

In this chapter we have emphasized the need for classroom teachers to adopt a range of assessment processes that are sensitive to the varying individual needs of a diverse group of students. These may include the following:

- Creation of student profiles that have sections corresponding to individual strengths and learning needs.
- Development of assessment systems that include the dimensions of the areas of the eight multiple intelligences: verbal-linguistic, logical-mathematical, bodily-kinesthetic, visual-spatial, musical-rhythmic, interpersonal, intrapersonal, and naturalistic.
- Implementation of the requirements of students' IEPs in assessment practices.
- Development of appropriate involvement from other teachers, professionals, paraprofessionals, students, and parents in decisions about assessments in the classroom.
- Analysis of assessments to ensure that adequate knowledge of the subject and knowledge about diverse learners are integrated.
- Development of a clear and consistent system that reflects decisions relating to what and why particular assessments are included.

We have discussed here the importance of the process of assessment for teaching in an inclusive classroom—assessment that celebrates diversity through the different strategies employed by the teacher in the classroom. The value of an assessment process that acknowledges the role of teacher knowledge of the subject/curriculum, teacher knowledge and understanding about the students in the class, the assessment principles and instructional practices of the teacher, and the relationship between the teacher and the student has been discussed. In the vignette at the beginning of the chapter, Miss Adams introduced the notion of differentiated assessment in the inclusive classroom in a simple but explicit way. The process of assessment in an inclusive classroom is indeed complex and varied. It should be seen as dynamic, evolving, and ever changing, depending on the subject knowledge and group of learners. It is a process that should be shared among teachers, students, and parents. In this way we can develop a community of learning in the classroom that has assessment at its heart, not to confirm failure, but to inform future teaching and learning for students who learn differently.

PART TWO

Practical Applications

In this section the discussion of practical applications of varied classroom processes gives substance to the previous contextual section. The particular focus is on performance assessment, assessment of students who are culturally and linguistically diverse learners, and on using informal assessments in literacy. The overriding message from all these chapters is that of using research-based strategies to inform decisions about assessment practices. Through the discussions presented, the importance of flexibility and creativity in the choice of assessment processes is highlighted. In considering the range of practical tools discussed through the chapters, teachers, school leaders, and administrators can gain a greater appreciation of the reality of the multiple forms of assessment. Through the informed adoption of such assessment strategies, tools that are responsive to individual, group, and curriculum demands can be created, to inform instruction in a meaningful way.

Performance Assessment in the Elementary Grades

*Stephen Rushton and
Anne Marie Juola-Rushton*

Early Monday morning, several students from a multiage 3rd- to 5th-grade class burst into their classroom in anticipation of what new projects await their discovery. Recent visits to both the local landfill and the city's wastewater treatment center have excited their curiosity. They know that a new unit on pollution is on the horizon, and they are eager to see what their teacher has prepared for them. The room has learning centers offering a variety of materials and experiences. An underwater scene, designed and painted by the students, is superimposed on the windows. Six tables are arranged in communities of four houses with ships' masts made from 6" cardboard tubing. Each mast is mounted with rigging, and a flag representing each community's name hangs above the sail. Student stories, chosen as exemplars through a peer review assessment process, line the cupboards, bulletin boards, and walls, demonstrating students' newfound knowledge of ocean life and the elements of the writing process. Chattering among the students concludes with their decisions of what center to approach first. Some are working on editing articles for the classroom newspaper, others are finishing their personal reflections of the ocean unit in their learning logs, and a few are beginning to work on creating a group landfill. A focused hum of learning suffuses the room.

Just outside the door the principal is speaking to the classroom teacher. A child hears the principal say, "You know I support your teaching style, but my hands are tied. Due to the newly adopted statewide Comprehensive Assessment Tests, the superintendent is being pressured to demonstrate accountability." After a short pause he concludes, "You might want to think about teaching toward the test and spending less time doing projects."

Educators at all levels, and especially elementary school teachers, are being challenged by such dilemmas, which can cause internal stress for teachers, undermine school reform, and even contribute to inappropriate teaching practices (Harrington-Lueker, 1991). State-level accountability tests must be balanced with a rich assortment of high-quality assessments at the school and classroom levels to provide an overall picture of student performance. Such embedded classroom assessments must be aligned to desired learning expectations and to effective current teaching practices. There are many assessment tools that a teacher can choose to employ, including anecdotal teacher note taking, structured observations (with or without a rating scale), individual and group projects, teacher- and student-prepared tests, student portfolios, and written reports.

THE RELATIONSHIP BETWEEN
THE BRAIN, LEARNING, AND ASSESSMENT

One purpose of assessment is to aid teachers in the gathering of information that helps them gain insights regarding how and what their children understand and are learning. Adams (1998) succinctly connects the importance of assessment to learning, stating that "assessment is integral to teaching and learning, and it plays a major role in how and what we teach, and in how and what children learn" (p. 220). The purpose of using any form of assessment is to provide clarity about the learner's strengths and to inform the teacher about any area of growth that may need attention. Assessment not only provides an understanding of the learner's needs, it is also about informing teachers about how their instruction and the curriculum are evolving. Assessing the achievement performance of the elementary child is a complex task because the child is ever changing, building upon prior knowledge as new information is gained. As children gain a greater understanding of the world around them, no one assessment tool can gauge the changes; rather, a combination of assessments can address the evolution of knowledge. The use of formal and informal evaluative tools is important in every elementary classroom, as no single assessment tool meets the demands of all types of learning, the nature of all teaching styles, or the needs of every child in all subject areas.

The child's cognitive-affective and emotional processes need to be matched by a rich learning environment that stimulates the brain's reasoning and higher-order functions. Research in the field of neuroscience (Diamond & Hopson, 1998; Sylwester, 1997) demonstrates a clear and different insight of the learning process and the importance of exposing the learner to a wide variety of environmental sensory stimuli.

The brain is a highly complex organ with many dynamic processes working simultaneously, among them memory, attention, and recall. This has clear implications for the dynamics of and interplay between the learning process, the learning environment, and assessment processes. The brain works as an integrated whole, as various neurotransmitters and endorphins either increase or decrease the learner's ability to process information. Educators (e.g., Caine & Caine, 1997; Gardner, 1993; Jensen, 1998; Rushton, 2001; Rushton, Eitelgeorge, & Zickafoose, 2003) are connecting these new insights on how the brain works to the learning environment; and they indicate that stress and high-interest factors can affect a student's ability to process information.

An educator's job is to create classroom learning environments that optimize the brain's ability to absorb and retain information and then to match the assessment tools to these practices. This is done by first creating safe, exciting, and rigorous learning environments that fully immerse children in an integrated, relevant curriculum that requires manipulating concrete objects and solving problems in real-life situations. The vignette at the beginning of the chapter portrays students finishing up an ocean unit and beginning a study on pollution. The room is filled with projects that help the children to integrate their thinking. Teachers now need a process that records and evaluates their performance in this setting. In the ocean unit, this takes the form of ongoing, embedded assessment on circumferences, addition, problem solving, and measurement in mathematics, as well as a variety of writing skills. Such a multidimensional approach to curriculum and learning leads naturally to a multidimensional approach to assessment. Since the brain does not simply store all information in one region but connects one area to another, so should our assessment.

PERFORMANCE-BASED ASSESSMENT EMBEDDED IN PRACTICE

> If there's a hot item on the burner of school reform, it's alternatives to standardized testing. And if there's a front-runner in the race to provide a more accurate accounting of your students' strengths and weaknesses, it is performance-based assessment [of] so-called higher-order thinking skills many believe are beyond the reach of multiple-choice items. (Harrington-Lueker, 1991, p. 20)

Incorporating daily performance-based assessment practices into the classroom through, for example, the use of observations, checklists, rubrics, journaling, and portfolios offers valuable strategies and tools for a systematic and focused approach to embedded performance-based assessments.

Observations and Record Keeping

Observation and record keeping of the child's learning can be a powerful assessment tool when employed in a systemic way. Waite-Stupiansky
(1997) suggests that observations can take the form of the teacher either
listening to the student's interaction with the environment or questioning
the student's educational choices. It is a challenge for a teacher to record
effectively student learning in a busy and active classroom. Observation
schedules, similar to that illustrated in Figure 3.1, offer a valuable tool in
the process of collecting observations in a focused and manageable way.

In using the schedule, a teacher is able to record pertinent information
directly related to the desired student learning. In the suggested format,
a teacher completes the standards/objectives and instructional-strategies
sections before the learning takes place. During the learning, student
responses and performance are completed, in quantitative or qualitative
ways. The observation schedule offers an example of a quantitative recording key that is helpful in managing teacher responses. Here teachers apply
a letter code key such as "M" for *mastery*, "I" for *introduced*, and "S" for
struggling. A third column is included to record additional comments—for
example, information on individual student response to collaborative peer
groupings or student response to a particular teaching strategy. Providing
students themselves with the observation schedule offers them opportunities to participate in their own assessment and clarifies the nature of the
record keeping that teachers are completing on them. Information col-
lated on the observation schedules can be used for further lesson planning
from the perspective of the standards/objectives of the lesson focus or
other classroom-management issues. Collecting and analyzing observation records can be time consuming, and their management needs to be
carefully structured and paced by the teacher. This pacing can be achieved
through focusing observations upon a certain number of students in a
particular class period and focusing observation upon a certain number of
standards/objectives in a particular class period.

The use of handheld devices to input observational data can also lead
to a more efficient use of teacher time. Checklists composed of developmental standards-based objectives can also provide a simplified, more
immediate format for observational assessment. Recorded over time, the
student's growth can be supported through color-coding each milestone's
mastery, supplying documentation of each accomplishment. Observation
schedules, however organized, provide a valid means of evaluating stu-

dents' ongoing learning, especially when observation data are collected regularly and systematically, consisting of objective and specific descriptions of children's behaviors tied to the objectives and standards that focus upon the desired learning (Cunningham & Allington, 2003).

FIGURE 3.1. Sample Observation Schedule for Ocean Unit

State Standards 3rd Grade	Instructional Strategy/ Classroom Organization	Student Performance (M = mastery, I = introduced, S = struggling)	Additional Comments and Date
MA.B.3.2.1 Solves real-world problems involving estimates of measurement of length and weight.	Captain's log inventory activity. Collaborative grouping based on preferred learning style.		
MA.B.3.2.1 Solves real-world problems involving estimates of measurement of area.	Mast-making activity. Collaborative grouping based on ability.		
MA.A.4.2.1 Uses estimation strategies in problem solving and computation.	Preparation activity for role-play journey across ocean. Collaborative grouping based on student choice.		
LA.B.2.2.1 Writes notes, comments, and observations that reflect comprehension of content and experiences from a variety of media.	Individual oral and visual presentations to group on self-chosen ocean project.		
LA.B.2.2.3 Writes for a variety of occasions, audiences, and purposes.	Poetry writing challenge in mixed-ability pairs.		

A clear illustration of learning can be gained through the observation of the representations that students make in their own writings each day. Journals, word-study notebooks, and science observation logs are just a few forms of natural documentation. These written forms provide not only accountability for students and teachers but also a connection to learning objectives for the educator, as well as a tangible product that illustrates student ability.

Involving students in performance-based assessment embedded in practice allows a unique perspective on learning. When students are able to take ownership of their learning and assessment, their academic attempts increase (Reeves, 2004). Teachers can structure student involvement in performance-based assessment so that the process is meaningful, manageable, and focused. One way to accomplish this is through structuring student reflections by questions. For example, a standards-based objective for an aspect of the ocean unit relates to the development of problem solving. Adapted from self- and peer-evaluation work from the Alaska Department of Education (1996), students can be asked the following questions to prompt and guide their reflections of a learning activity they have completed:

- How did you get started? What were your first thoughts?
- Did you use any problem-solving strategies discussed in class? Which ones? How did they help you?
- How did you find your solution?
- Did you try anything that did not work? How did you feel about it?
- Did you find a solution? How did you check your answer? How did you check the accuracy of your answer?

Through student responses to these prompt questions, teachers are offered a unique perspective of how individual students are making meaning of problem-solving strategies already taught in class. Students are being asked to reflect upon the application of such strategies in a particular learning context. Over time, as the teacher collects a series of these, a more comprehensive picture of student performance on standards relative to problem-solving is achieved.

The Role of Rubrics in Performance-Based Assessment

Rubric formats based on standards-based objectives can also be used as an effective assessment tool in a child-centered elementary classroom.

There are many rubric-generating sites on the Internet that a teacher can use to support rubric development. However, in employing scoring guides of this type, it is important to remember that the rubric should relate directly to the identified desired learning. In other words, it should assess what it is intended to assess. It is important that grades not be the scale for the rubric but that each score point on the rubric should be based on specific matched criteria.

Portfolio Assessment

A portfolio collection provides a potential structure to collate and evaluate the varied assessment forms generated and applied in a developmentally appropriate setting. Three major purposes exist in using the portfolio: assessment and evaluation, student assessment and self-reflection, and representation of educational progress. For the ocean unit described in the vignette at the start of this chapter, the data sheets encompassing work fulfillments, written documentation from oral presentations, student reflections of the experience, and photographs of completed projects are all possible types of documentation that the teacher could include when incorporating the portfolio into the classroom. As actual evidence of student learning, the portfolio provides a primary source of that learning. In a portfolio, assessment and teaching are so interrelated that the line between them often becomes blurred (Waite-Stupiansky, 1997). There are as many content possibilities for the portfolio as there are purposes. Organizational expectations and strategies offer and make manageable the process of building a portfolio. Figure 3.2 contains a range of portfolio types that a teacher may incorporate into teaching to assess and evaluate student learning.

Thus the variety of portfolio formats available to a teacher is large, and there is an important role for informed professional decision-making by the teacher in choosing which portfolio structure to adopt. Such decision making can be influenced by such factors as the standards/objectives being addressed in the learning, the nature of the learning context, and the partnership between student and teacher. One way to approach this is to include student choice in selecting exemplary samples of work related to specific standards/objectives from the rubric. Figure 3.3 shows a format for an assessment plan for the development of a portfolio that invites both teacher and student participation in the choice of exemplary student learning and achievement.

FIGURE 3.2. Possible Types of Portfolio

Portfolio Options	Purpose	Student or Teacher Collections
Display	Showcases classroom work or projects to exhibit student mastery	Student and/or Teacher
Evaluative	Contains assessments that guide instructional purposes	Teacher
Performance Based	Provides documentation of student's performance ability	Student and/or Teacher
Process Based	Documents a "work in progress" over a short or long period of time	Student
Developmental	Categorized by objective domains	Teacher
Subject Area	Track growth in each subject area	Student and/or Teacher
Individual	Envelops only the work done by the student independently	Student and/or Teacher
Partner or Group	Implemented for partner or group efforts toward common learning objectives	Students
Electronic	Consists of a compilation of pieces demonstrated through technology such as PowerPoint presentations, i-movies, or web pages	Student and/or Teacher
Aggregated	Draws from work of each student to compile a whole-class result	Students and/or Teacher
Archived	Passes from school year to school year throughout the student's academic endeavor	Teacher

The student's portfolio plays an important part in the teacher-parent conference as well as the overall assessment of the student's growth and accomplishments throughout the year. Although from year to year and from student to student selections chosen for the portfolio may change, the constancy of the portfolio and its valuable representation of the child's learning will always stay the same. According to Gober (2002), "Teachers are beginning to realize that this type of performance assessment gives a more accurate picture of who the child is, and how the child is growing and learning" (p. 4). Through implementation of student portfolios from the beginning of the school term as a part of the daily routine, students become an active participant in choosing documentation that supports their educational gains.

FIGURE 3.3. Assessment Plan for Embedded Portfolio Assessment

Instructional Activity and Standards	Student-Chosen Exemplar of Performance	Teacher-Chosen Exemplar of Performance
Captain's log inventory, MA.B.3.2.1	Inventory and peer review of inventory	Rubric scoring sheet for inventory
Mast-making activity, MA.B.3.2.1	Photographs of mast making showing use of measuring devices	Photographs plus student-completed mast-making estimation sheet
Role-play preparations, MA.A.4.2.1	Lists and notes on estimations of quantities of equipment needed for journey	Completed observation schedule for role-play preparation
Individual presentation, LA.B.2.2.1	Three pieces of student-chosen "best" work/achievement from project	One piece of teacher-chosen "best" work/achievement from project
Ocean life poem, L.A.B.2.2.3	Poem	Poem with teacher anecdotal notes relating to Standards

PRINCIPLES FOR CLASSROOM ASSESSMENT

We have argued in this chapter that in nurturing an elementary classroom that is child centered and that has an emphasis on discovery learning the teacher needs to develop assessments that

- Are sensitive to current brain-based research; for example, ones that build in perceptual, tactile, and auditory opportunities for students to demonstrate their learning;
- Employ real-life assessment opportunities that allow the students to engage with concrete objects in problem-solving scenarios;
- Use a variety of assessment tools, including observation schedules, checklists, rubrics, and portfolios, to embed assessment in the on-going curriculum while at the same time keeping it as objective as possible;
- Carefully structure the involvement of students in the collection of assessment and evaluation data;
- Use professional judgment to make key decisions in the choice of

portfolios that will help to ensure that assessment is embedded in classroom practice; and
• Employ portfolios in three ways: for assessment and evaluation, for student self-reflection, and for representation of progress.

For the classroom teacher in the vignette at the start of this chapter, pulling out the well-managed portfolios of his students, along with developing a well-prepared assessment plan, would provide bona fide verification of the curriculum being received. Substantiating practices with evidence of student performance through the validity of performance-based assessment will balance state assessments and demonstrate to administrators and parents the value of a learning-centered education. For students in the elementary grades, this sustains the discovery learning that engages the child's innate curiosity to learn.

"Can You Listen Faster?"

Assessment of Students Who Are Culturally and Linguistically Diverse Learners

Weimin Mo

> It has been a year and half since Juan, a 5th grader, and his family moved to this country. Juan's conversational English is so fluent that sometimes teachers forget that he is from Mexico. In math class, after Juan has asked Mr. Fitzgerald, the math teacher, a couple of times to slow down and explain a simple calculation process, Mr. Fitzgerald says half jokingly, "Can you listen faster?"

Some teachers spend the whole day with their students but do not really know or see them. Mr. Fitzgerald in the vignette is one of them. Listening-comprehension speed is affected by a number of factors, such as language proficiency, experiences in the past, background knowledge, content of the conversation, or cognitive demands of the task (Chiappe, Siegel, & Gottardo, 2002; Derwing & Munro, 2001; Major, Fitzmaurice, Bunta, & Balasubramanian, 2002). However, how these factors function in students who are culturally and linguistically diverse (CLD) varies from a student whose first language is English.

INTRODUCTION TO KEY ISSUES

For students who are Culturally and Linguistically Diverse (CLD), the ability to listen and comprehend what is heard is complicated by language used in past learning and life experiences. This is often juxtaposed with the English language and the mainstream culture in which students are learning in the present (Derwing & Munro, 2001; Major et al., 2002). Therefore, it is justifiable to ask how Mr. Fitzgerald is going to assess Juan's performance fairly, since the child is obviously unable to follow his teaching in class.

The diversity of the U.S. population is growing rapidly. It is estimated that by the year 2050, more than 40% of students will be racially and linguistically diverse (Cartledge & Loe, 2001). Presently 14% of students in grades K–12 speak a language other than English at home (Gonzalez, Brusca-Vega, & Yawkey, 1997), and approximately 2% of students between the ages of 5 and 17 have either limited English proficiency or do not speak English (U.S. Census Bureau, 2004). As a result, to help students who are CLD achieve their academic goals and become productive citizens of our society, teachers need to be armed with three types of knowledge (Blair, 2003, p. 69):

- Knowledge of essential learning in their subject areas;
- Knowledge of elements of effective teaching; and
- Knowledge of culturally responsive instructional practices.

Culturally responsive instructional practices are defined in this chapter as the type of teaching that is tailored according to how students' culture and language affect their understanding and learning. Assessment is an integral part of this instructional practice. To educators, assessment concerning students who are CLD involves not only collecting data on their performance, but also gathering information on how students' learning is affected by their culture and language and using it to tailor instruction and assessment to the individual student. This chapter highlights the need to understand the influence of students' culture and language on learning, to relate students' achievement orientation to instruction and assessment, and to include students' continuing motivation in assessment.

UNDERSTANDING THE INFLUENCE OF STUDENTS' LANGUAGE ON LEARNING

Culturally sensitive teachers actively learn the language and culture of their students and recognize that it is part of their job to provide the kind of cultural and linguistic validation that is missing in the society at large (Garcia, 2002). In reality, there is such a variety of languages spoken by today's students when they are not in school (U.S. Census Bureau, 2004) that it is impossible for teachers to learn all their languages. Mr. Fitzgerald's misconception illustrates this lack of experiences in second-language learning. A student may speak some English; however, this level of English-language acquisition and knowledge may not be enough to represent abilities accurately in an English-based assessment. Teachers must understand that it takes a considerable amount of time (5 to 10 years) before students who are CLD are able to think in English (Gonzalez, Brusca-Vega, & Yawkey, 1997). This situation inevitably affects the accuracy with which teachers are able to assess students' ability to learn in school and how they teach.

Recognizing Differences

It is important to remember that students who are CLD have varying levels of English proficiency, including non-English speaking, limited English speaking, and fluent English speaking. Careful observation of how such students use oral language may provide critical information for differentiated instruction and assessment. The following are some questions classroom teachers may use during observation to measure students' communicative proficiency concerning the major parts of comprehension, fluency, vocabulary, pronunciation, and grammar.

1. How well can the student understand class conversations and discussions: very little, only when others speak slowly, with much repetition, or with only some repetition?
2. When the student speaks, does the speech sound halting and fragmentary, hesitant, or interrupted? Does the student often lapse into word searches? Has the student ever initiated a conversation at all?
3. Is academic conversation with the student possible? Does the student often misuse words? Does the student often rephrase because of limited vocabulary?
4. Is it difficult to understand what the student says? Does the student repeat him- or herself often? Do you have to listen closely when the student talks? Does his or her speech sometimes cause misunderstandings?
5. Does the student frequently make errors with grammar and stick to simple sentence patterns?

Linguistic differences can adversely affect a written assessment, as students who are culturally diverse learners will have to translate back and forth in their mind from English to their native language or vice versa. For instance, if the word *cat* appears in a sentence, a Spanish-speaking child may have to translate it into "*gato.*" In order to comprehend what he or she reads, the child will also have to rearrange the sentence according to Spanish word order and adjust its inflectional ending according to its number, gender, or position in the sentence. The switching not only slows down the student's reading, but also draws on extra cognitive resources that the student needs for processing content area information. To minimize these influences, nonverbal assessment strategies can be used. Students can physically demonstrate their responses, for example, by pointing to the correct answer. Another nonverbal assessment is using pictures or illustrations. For example, if Juan is learning about photosynthesis, he can illustrate the process rather than explain it verbally.

The Role of Cognition

Cognition largely relies on our language capability. Teachers such as Mr. Fitzgerald are not consciously aware that each CLD student's language capability in learning varies greatly depending on how language and cognitive experiences interact in the child's past learning. In some areas, such as everyday conversation, these students can more rapidly respond and process the information because the vocabulary is simpler and more repetitive. Technically, this is called contextualized language, meaning it uses many physical cues in a face-to-face situation (Garcia, 2002). However, in subject areas such as math, they must analyze the vocabulary, translate certain words for meaning into their first language, and then cognitively process the task (Shrum & Glisan, 2004).

Juan learned how to count only in Spanish, and his acquisition of math concepts has been processed entirely in his first language. To learn mathematical concepts in English, Juan will proceed through several steps. First, he will translate the material into his native language, Spanish. This may require looking up a word in a Spanish dictionary. Next, he will cognitively process the information. If the material contains new concepts or cultural references, he may need to do background learning such as asking questions or looking up material in an encyclopedia. His final step is to translate the material back into English. This process requires Mr. Fitzgerald to reduce his rate of speech so that Juan can keep up with the math lesson, since the type of language used for instruction is decontextualized language, in which in thinking and communication the learner has to rely on cognitive cues that are more abstract.

Albert Einstein once made the following statement: "People slowly accustomed themselves to the idea that the physical states of space itself were the final physical reality" (1929). In spite of the fact that we know every word of the sentence, we really don't understand what he was talking about unless we have background knowledge in physics. The reason that the remark doesn't make sense to us is because there is no interaction between the professional language and our cognitive learning. That means that the academic discourse can be understood only after we have repeatedly used it in our academic cognitive involvement so that our thinking is geared to the language, with its special meanings embedded only in the cognitive process of the specific area. Cognitively complex learning always involves repetitively playing with the highly specialized code.

LANGUAGE ACQUISITION AND LANGUAGE LEARNING

Language acquisition and language learning are two different processes and need to be considered discretely when assessing students. Language acquisition is subconscious, effortless, and involuntary. It accounts for our language proficiency and is mainly responsible for both our fluency and our accuracy in language (Krashen, 2003). As a Chinese American I was once was asked, "What language do you speak when you talk to your family members and other relatives?" Reflecting on all the facts of my life, I was surprised to realize that it all depended on the topic of the conversation. When I tried to discuss things such as cars or computers, I always spoke English, even with my relatives. That is because driving and using computers are the things I learned to do in English. I felt awkward or even at a loss to search for the right words to express myself in my native language. Experiences tell us that language acquisition and cognitive learning cannot be separated from each other.

The functional use of language, our conscious language learning, is very limited, and its role in language is a conscious monitor of error correction provided it does not interfere with communication (Krashen, 2003). There is only one way to learn the language, that is, "when we understand the message . . . when we understand what we hear or what we read" (p. 4). Therefore, for classroom teachers, the key to effectively teaching students who are CLD learners is to assess their communicative competence in the specific content area. For instance, before a new lesson is taught, classroom teachers need to check whether the students have a sufficient vocabulary, both general and special, to follow and to be involved in class discussion. If Mr. Fitzgerald is teaching the class about fractions, he should have a visual depiction of a fraction in the classroom. On this visual, the vocabulary terms *numerator* and *denominator* should be clearly identified. This will provide Juan with the proper vocabulary for the lesson. Another good practice is to determine whether the students have appropriate syntactical knowledge to express themselves and understand others in class discussion. Many teachers put students who are CLD learners on the spot by asking them questions in front of their classmates. This causes anxiety for the students, particularly for those who are at an early English language–proficiency stage. Simply asking a student "Do you understand?" may elicit a yes, even if the student does not comprehend the material (Haynes & O'Loughlin, 1999b). Evaluate their listening comprehension skills by asking simple questions that will elicit a one- or two-word response in a one-on-one discussion (Haynes & O'Loughlin, 1999a). "How" or "why" questions can be asked of students who are more linguistically advanced. Activities that allow students to point to the correct answer will also illustrate comprehension. Finally, it is imperative that the teacher identifies whether the students who are CLD have sufficient linguistic knowledge to accomplish assignments and read the textbooks independently. Many such assessments become a measure of a student's linguistic ability rather than a measure of content knowledge or skill (Ascher, 1990). Therefore, a teacher should build background knowledge by providing visuals, graphic organizers, and vocabulary lists (Haynes & O'Loughlin, 1999a).

Content area teachers should pay attention not only to students' reading but also to all areas of language reception and use (Haynes & O'Loughlin, 1999a, 1999b). In other words, linguistic and academic cognitive involvements are so closely interwoven that they are reciprocal in subject areas. For that reason, what Mr. Fitzgerald teaches and assesses does not help Juan at all either in language or in math. Of course, how to coordinate the two aspects of our teaching represents an interesting challenge.

Recent research (Garcia, 2002) has introduced some strategies that assist in making instruction more understandable and assessment more effective. Figure 4.1 lists some activities a teacher may use to adapt the assessment based on recent research. For example, one strategy is to simplify but not artificially restrict language structures. Mr. Fitzgerald can use shorter sentences with simple syntax that are easier for Juan to understand. Communications should include unambiguous terminology, as well as provide descriptions and examples rather than definitions. A second strategy is to contextualize both oral and written texts with pictures, charts, and diagrams. For example, Mr. Fitzgerald can label all the stages of a butterfly's life cycle on a bulletin board. The words can also be translated into the student's native language and appear under the English word. This will, in turn, help Juan learn the vocabulary and teach Mr. Fitzgerald and the other students a different language. A third strategy is to provide for repeated access to ideas and vocabulary. Mr. Fitzgerald can provide several handouts and charts about the butterfly's life cycle. He can also provide library books and magazines that show butterfly stages. The final strategy recommended by Garcia (2002) is to create a structure that allows for both comprehension and the need to act on and talk about content. The use of both formative and summative assessment techniques allows this to happen. If Juan is creating a travel brochure about Mexico, his native country, he can turn in each draft to Mr. Fitzgerald for feedback. This will allow Mr. Fitzgerald to clarify the facts and gauge Juan's literacy skills. It will also allow Mr. Fitzgerald to learn about Juan's background. Another effective tool for evaluating product and process is the use of portfolio assessments.

FIGURE 4.1. Sample Activities Adopted for Culturally Responsive Assessment

Research-Based Strategies	Examples of Adaptation
STRATEGY 1 Simplifying language structure to save cognitive resources	1) Using short sentences and simple syntax in speech. 2) Using cloze paragraphs in assessment. 3) Providing sufficient examples. 4) Asking students to act out their interpretation. 5) Asking students to perform a scene. 6) Using the arts as a form of assessment.
STRATEGY 2 Contextualizing oral and written texts	1) Using objects related to key concepts. 2) Using learning centers as a form of assessment. 3) Providing words of key concepts in native language. 4) Teacher modeling the task first.
STRATEGY 3 Repeated access to key ideas and vocabulary	1) Providing word walls or word lists. 2) Asking students to make visuals for self-help. 3) Using multimedia assignments. 4) Providing extra time.
STRATEGY 4 Creating interactive structures for assessment	1) Using group presentation with multiple roles. 2) Providing individual support.

UNDERSTANDING THE INFLUENCE OF
STUDENTS' CULTURE ON LEARNING

A teacher, often in an unconscious way, assumes that the student possesses the same conceptual system that the teacher does, even though the student obviously uses a different grammar and some strange words. The teacher then attempts to assess and teach with reference to such a presumed shared conceptual system. It can become difficult for a student to process the task. We need to remind ourselves constantly that students who are CLD do not necessarily share the same knowledge or life experiences (Abrams, Ferguson, & Laud, 2001; Laing & Kamhi, 2003). For example, if the objects we use as examples in teaching and assessment are not familiar to some of our students, chances are they may not cognitively process the learning as easily as other students. For instance, when I taught primary grades in Pennsylvania, my former colleagues and I realized how our choice of objects for examples might make a difference in children's conceptual understanding. In teaching students who are CLD, especially those from developing countries where automobiles were still not a popular transportation tool, we found that when we used automobiles as an example to ask children to categorize items by size, color, and shape, the children who were newly immigrated from developing countries took a surprisingly longer time than mainstream students to categorize cars despite the fact that they were able to process similar cognitive learning activities, such as blocks, in about the same time, or even faster, than many mainstream peers. They seemed to have more difficulty telling cars' different sizes even though they had visual contact with them just moments before they were asked to categorize. Their cultural experiences have perceptually predisposed them how to organize their sensations: what and how to attend to, or simply ignore.

A classic example of how socioculture and language affect students' perceptions is the use of pictures as teaching devices. Pictures are not a universal language. How children respond to pictures or interpret their visual input has a lot to do with the children's past experiences and language. The language of the classroom is a highly specialized code and it is appropriate that the universal notion of "developmentally appropriate approaches" should be revised to recognize the more specific "culturally and linguistically appropriate" developmental issues (Cohen & Pompa, 1996). We need to keep these issues in mind constantly and check how we instruct and assess our students in light of students' past sociocultural experiences as well as literacy development.

Culture "provides the standard for perceiving, believing, evaluating, communicating, and acting among those who share a language, a historic period, or a geographic location" (Triandis, 1996, p. 408). Most classroom teachers seldom realize that they speak and write English using a kind of old-tale shorthand and that the language is heavily laden with subtle suggestions to meanings that are deeply rooted in our culture. Language is embedded in the culture (Jacobs & Tunnell, 2004) and our assessment in classrooms must be sensitive to this. I once recommended *Harry Potter* to a middle school student with an Asian cultural background, thinking that at his reading level he should be able to handle far more difficult books than a 5th grade–level novel such as *Harry Potter*. However, the next day the student came back and returned the book without finishing it. He told me that after the first few pages he had felt overwhelmed by copious descriptions that did not make sense to him, so he decided that the book did not interest him.

RELATING STUDENTS' ACHIEVEMENT MOTIVATION
TO INSTRUCTION AND ASSESSMENT

In considering culturally responsive assessment practices, there are two important questions that are related to students' cultures and motivation to learn: First, to what extent does culture affect students' motivation to learn, and how can we build our expectations of students' performance on solid, realistic ground so students' performance can improve on a predictably steady basis? Second, what do we need to know about the changes most students who are CLD go through, and how can we help them effectively?

We are all products of our past experiences and present conditions. Classroom teachers have some existential knowledge of how sociocultural factors influence the orientation of children's achievement. The critical importance of family dynamics and role relationships has an impact on a student's cultural motivation to learn. For example, certain Asian child-rearing experiences and the Asian family structure have some bearing on Asian American students' motivation toward achievement. Such students are taught from early childhood to view their role within the family and society in terms of relationships and obligations. Asian children develop a sense of moral obligation and primary loyalty to their family. Their cultural beliefs dictate that only continual achievements that maintain and enhance the family name are considered acceptable (Morrow, 1991). This clearly has an impact on the students' motivation to learn in the classroom. However, some cultural beliefs and practices may not be so aligned to the academic structures and studies in our schools. Our schools are all future-oriented institutions, which means that what we are learning is preparation for our lives in the future. Not all people in the world tie their lives so closely to the future. For example, in Mexican culture the significant time is the *present*. The family does not typically save what they make in order to buy what they need in the future. If a child grows up with this kind of notion of time, it may influence the child's motivation to achieve in our future-oriented schools.

There are things we can do to create an environment that will help foster and assess student achievement motivation (Garcia, 2002):

- Beware the values that are based on lopsided views of social status, ethnicity, language, and so forth, which will lead to such situations as the overrepresentation of Anglo-Americans in gifted classes and of minorities in learning disability programs.
- Develop the ability of school staff to communicate effectively in languages other than English.
- Use evaluation processes that embrace other cultures and languages, particularly at the beginning stages of reading, instead of mandatory assessment in English regardless of students' communicative competence.
- Challenge the *"el pobrecito"* syndrome that leads teachers to believe that these children just need a safe and loving place, not challenging curriculum.

It is no easy job to alter students' achievement orientation. American education has always been about educating students who are CLD, acculturating and merging them into the mainstream culture. A contemporary difference is that we are now dealing with a much wider range of diversity and a much larger number of students. In spite of the fact that motivation orientation is something shaped early in our childhood, it can be transformed.

THE ROLE OF STUDENTS' MOTIVATION IN ASSESSMENT

Many of us have met charismatic teachers who know which button to push in order to motivate us. They are so inspiring that there seems to be magic in their voices, and whatever they say can elicit and maximize all the motivation predispositions we still have inside and push us to strive for achievement. In creating an achievement environment, all inspiring teachers know that they must set high expectations for their students, whether they state these expectations loudly and clearly or merely imply them in their requirements.

Key questions emerge about how teachers guide students to fulfill expectations. When we lay down stepping stones for students, how far apart from each other should we place them? How do the students feel about jumping onto the next stone? How do their previous experiences affect their determination to jump or precondition them in unfavorable ways? The level of challenge and the student's psychological preparation for the challenge are certainly critical in our assessment and are directly related to the success of our teaching. Moreover, we not only need to help build students' confidence with plentiful opportunities for success but also need to challenge some of their negative motivation predispositions. For example, in the long run, achievement motivation is the key to their success. We define achievement motivation as the eagerness and persistence to work to their potential no matter what.

In order to get thoughts of achievement into students' minds, classroom teachers need to encourage students to explore the theme of achievement and reflect on how they feel when they have accomplished something. Teachers need to assess when the moment is right to bring up the topic. Achievement is not a difficult topic to connect to things that students encounter in their lives, especially the success of children like themselves or from similar backgrounds. The discussion could be about their personal successful experiences or those of others. Teachers should guide students in exploring how and why people can achieve success. They can also discuss how high achievers behave or discipline themselves. Teachers can talk to students about what they think their own achievement potential is. Whenever a task is assigned, teachers should check a student's motivation in relation to the task.

To provide sufficiently challenging tasks for students so that they may have authentic opportunities to succeed, teachers need to assess students' knowledge base and learning skills while at the same time assessing how students' current predisposition for achievement interact with relevant sociocultural influences.

IMPLICATIONS FOR CLASSROOM ASSESSMENT

In this chapter I have emphasized the need for classroom teachers to adopt a range of assessment processes that are sensitive to the varying needs of students who are culturally and linguistically diverse. These include:

- Providing classroom assessments that are sensitive to the first language of the student;
- Providing classroom assessments that validate the culture of the student;
- Developing classroom assessments that consider language acquisition and language learning discretely;
- Developing classroom assessments that are sensitive to the relationship between the students' cognition, language, and culture;
- Developing culturally responsive assessment tools; and
- Developing classroom assessments that consider motivational factors in a culturally sensitive way.

Teaching and assessing students who are culturally and linguistically different presents many challenges and opportunities. The number of students from culturally and linguistically diverse backgrounds is increasing in our schools. In addition to carrying out regular assessment of students' performance on academic tasks, teachers need to understand and assess how the interactions of students' culture, language, and cognition affect their learning in the classroom, and assess how students' motivation to learn is complicated by their sociocultural experiences in the past and in the current cultural conditions. Teachers also need to understand and assess how effectively they can foster students' continuing motivation to achieve. It is in classrooms employing these guidelines that the assessment of Juan and his classmates will be most accurate and meaningful.

Using Informal Assessments to Monitor and Support Literacy Progress

Janice S. Eitelgeorge, G. Pat Wilson, and Karen Kent

Hurrying down the school hallway, 1st-year teacher Jennifer reaches Mrs. Berger, a 22-year veteran teacher. "Mrs. Berger, I really could use your help. I'm so worried about some of the children in my class, particularly Eric. He seems to be so far behind the others in reading and writing." Beginning teachers gravitate toward Mrs. Berger, with her ready smile and willingness to nurture new teachers. "Why don't you stay after school one night next week," Mrs. Berger replies, "I'll share a few assessment ideas. We will figure out where your children are and how you can help them progress. We can focus on Eric first. You will recognize some of these assessments from your university classes, so it should be fairly easy. Every year, I have some children who just worry me to death. I know just how you feel."

Mrs. Berger is a lifelong learner who has completed her master's degree in reading but continues to attend postgraduate classes, literacy workshops, and national conferences and has a practitioner library that is the envy of many teachers. She recognizes the importance of teachers' making instructional decisions based on the level of students' literacy development. Drawing from her practitioner library, she uses sound, research–based informal assessments that have been developed to identify children's understandings within several conceptual areas of literacy. The assessments can be used with readers for whom English is a second language, readers who appear to be struggling, and readers who are progressing well. Based on findings from such informal literacy assessments, Mrs. Berger provides her learners with appropriate instruction. In this chapter we share some of the informal literacy assessments that Mrs. Berger reviews with Jennifer.

Reading and writing are complex processes that call for multiple layers of assessment. Formal assessments that are used for program and policy decisions often boil down children's reading to a number that obscures understanding of individual differences and thereby misrepresents readers (Wilson, Martens, & Arya, 2005). Individual children have varied experiences in building literacy and therefore demonstrate different patterns of knowledge and understanding. Informal assessments help teachers see the pattern for each child and adjust instruction accordingly.

INFORMAL LITERACY ASSESSMENTS

The Literacy Assessment Checklist (Eitelgeorge, 2002; Eitelgeorge & Kent, 2001) is something Mrs. Berger uses in order to share a variety of informal literacy assessments with Jennifer. The checklist (see Figure 5.1 for a completed checklist) is organized into two broad categories, or domains, of development: *conceptual understanding of words* and the broader *reading-writing processes*. Within each domain are multiple assessments that help identify patterns in children's learning and track progress along developmental continua. In the list below, assessments used with each domain are delineated, along with references that can be used in seeking further information. Jennifer, the teacher in the vignette at the start of this chapter, can use any of the informal assessments at any point in the year to monitor and check an individual child's progress in each domain. In addition, she can assess all her children, at selected intervals during the school year, to create a classroom composite.

Domain 1: Conceptual Understandings of Words

- Phonemic awareness (Adams, 1994/1996; Yopp, 1995);
- Alphabetic principle/letter-sound correspondences (Clay, 2002);
- Concept of word (Downing & Oliver, 1973; Morris, 1981);
- Concepts of print (Bialystok, Shenfield, & Codd, 2000);
- Word knowledge through invented spelling (Bear, Invernizzi, Templeton, & Johnston, 2004; Ganske, 2000; Henderson, 1990; Read, 1975); and
- Receptive and expressive vocabulary (Readence, Bean, & Baldwin, 1995).

FIGURE 5.1. Literacy Assessment Checklist

FIRST GRADE

Student: Eric   **Date:** January 13

Synthesis of Progress and Instructional Recommendations

Comments: Eric read a Level 6 (unfamiliar text) instructionally for the Running Record. He should be reading at Instructional Level 9 by this time of the year to be considered "on grade level." Several other areas are below benchmark for this time of year. Hard worker; willing to learn. Check into possible speech problem—sounds and tendency to stutter—may affect literacy.

Instructional Strategies: Work with Eric in Shared and Guided Reading with Instructional Level 6, Alphabetic Principle, Speech to Print Match, Letter Identification, and Concepts of Print. Teach prediction, rereading, and summarization skills for comprehension. Continue instruction on cueing system for unknown words. Allow ample opportunities for independent level reading time, below Level 6, encourage both fiction and nonfiction. Check for possible speech problem—articulation, s, r, d. Word Study: blends, digraphs, long vowels with silent e markers, preconsonantal nasals, open and closed sorts. Writing—encourage more expansive writing.

Conceptual Understandings of Words

Phonemic Awareness
Benchmark is by mid-1st grade for on-grade level readers. 16 of 22 (75%)
Comments: Has difficulty hearing blends and segmentation of three phoneme words, instead breaks into two sounds, onset and rime for example, /r/ed/ and /j/ob/.

Alphabet Survey
Number correct 54 of 56 (96%)
Comments: September, 36 of 56 = 64%; should have been 70%
(a) name – unfamiliar with q and y
(b) sound – speech problem /s/, /r/, /d/
(c) word – not for q and y

Speech to Print Match
Levels: (1)____ (2)____ (3) X (4)____
Benchmark Notations: Should be a level 4.

Concepts of Print
Number correct 13 of 18
Benchmark Notations: Needs work on comma, quotation marks, two letters together, framing one and two words.

Developmental Spelling (Attach spelling inventory)
Emergent: _____ Letter Name: X (middle) Within Word Pattern: _____
Syllables and Affixes: _____ Derivational Relations: _____
Benchmark Notations: Review blends and digraphs. Introduce long vowels with silent-e markers. Work on preconsonantal nasals and blends. Check on speech problem with /s/, /r/, /d/.

Teacher Anecdotal Record of Receptive and Expressive Vocabulary
Understands word meanings and uses a well-developed vocabulary to express himself. Uses these skills to help comprehension. Check with speech teacher for sounds and stuttering tendency that may impact literacy.

(continued)

FIGURE 5.1. (continued)

READING AND WRITING PROCESSES

Reading Development Using a Running Record (Attach running record forms)
Instructional Reading Level: _6_ (_90%_); _____ (__%); _____ (__%); _____ (__%)
Books or Text Used and Date: The Seed (unfamiliar), January 13
Strengths of the cueing system: Eric's fluency developing with generally strong phrasing, denoting understanding of the text. Good use of expression. Strong semantic and syntactic cueing.

Weaknesses of the cueing system: Eric does not use rereading strategy to assist self-correction. Instead mumbles, hoping no one will notice, rather than using graphophonic cueing system. If after rereading he cannot predict using his semantic and syntactic cueing, he needs to look at the initial sound and ending chunk or rime, which correlates with his "late letter name" level. Speech problem with /r/ sound and ending sounds /s/ and /d/.

Oral Fluency Continuum

Emerging:_____ Developing:_X_ Gaining Fluency:_____ Fluent:_____
Comments: Beginning to read expressively by chunking the text into three- to four-word phrases. His pace is moderately slow on a first reading but progressively speeds up with repeated readings. Some rough spots with extended hesitations occur with low rate of self-correction.

Retelling Continuum

Emerging:_____ Developing:_X_ Gaining Competency:_____ Competent:_____
Comments: Partial retelling. Prompting assisted him to retell more than he initially had offered, which was a brief beginning with characters and setting, only a portion of the sequent events, and a terse ending. No details or descriptions were offered unless he was prompted to tell more about a specific scene. Then, he could describe the scene. However, he could not order the events.

Comprehension Interview (Scored 1-4 and any notations with response)
Self-Monitors: _2_ Summarizes: _2_ Infers: _2_ Connects: _2_ Predicts: _3_ Visualizes: _2_
Questions: _1; help Eric think as he reads_

Writing Development Continuum (Attach writing samples)
(1) Frozen-in-time___ (2) Illustrations with labels___
(3) Telegraphic message ___ (4) Approximations of sentences _X_
(5) Minimal retellings ___ (6) Patterned texts ___
(7) Attribute books___ (8) Limited sequence in chaining events____
(9) Sequence and chaining dominates___ (10) Focused chaining of events _____
(11) Rudimentary narratives ____ (12) Primitive narratives ____
Comments: Has many ideas that he wants to share but cannot hold in mind the numerous sentences as he struggles to spell and use letter-sound correspondences. Must continue to prompt him to reread after stretching each word to help him continue his thought processes. More prewriting talk to develop his sense of voice and use of storybook language.

Note. From Eitelgeorge (2002). Adapted with permission of the author.

Domain 2: Reading and Writing Processes

- Running records to identify strengths and weaknesses of the cueing systems and instructional reading level (Clay, 2002; Goodman, Watson, & Burke, 1987);
- Reading fluency (Zutell & Rasinski, 1991);
- Oral retelling and anecdotal comprehension checks (Applebee, 1979; Eitelgeorge, 1994; Hasan, 1984);
- Comprehension Interview (Harvey & Goudvis, 2000; Keene & Zimmermann, 1997); and
- Writing development (Eitelgeorge & Barrett, 2004).

The lists within the two domains offer a menu from which a teacher can choose assessments depending upon what aspect of literacy is in question. By creating a profile from the results, teachers can plan instruction to facilitate and monitor progress throughout the year. The basic procedure for creating a profile is to do the following:

1. Assess, using the informal assessments;
2. Analyze and interpret the results, recording results and notes on the checklist;
3. Apply the findings to instructional decisions;
4. Reflect on individual progress to reinforce or modify instruction; and
5. Reassess to monitor progress, recording results on the checklist to show progress.

The following sections provide more details on assessing the domains of *conceptual understanding of words* and of *reading and writing processes*. Incorporated into these sections are points made by Mrs. Berger regarding how Jennifer can use these assessments in her quest to improve instruction. Jennifer starts with Eric, one of her 1st graders (see Figure 5.1 for results).

CONCEPTUAL UNDERSTANDING OF WORDS

Phonemic Awareness

Phonemic awareness is an understanding that speech is composed of a series of individual sounds or phonemes; for example, the word *duck* contains three phonemes: /d/u/k/ (Adams, 1994/1996; Yopp, 1995). Phonemic awareness requires children to shift their cognitive attention from the content of speech in order to analyze or manipulate the sounds or phonemes in a word. This awareness is developed through playful activities that progress from matching, isolating, blending, adding, substituting, and segmenting phonemes. An assessment in this area is the Yopp–Singer Test of Phoneme Segmentation (Yopp, 1995), which is designed to be gamelike, with 22 words for children to break apart into individual sounds. Jennifer administered the Yopp–Singer to Eric. She found that he had difficulty separating blends and could not segment short words into each phoneme. He broke them into two sounds, an onset and rime, such as *r-ed*.

Assessing Alphabetic Principle

An assessment of the alphabetic principle gathers information about a child's understandings of the alphabet, including the letter names, sounds, and words that begin with the same letter or sound. Clay (2002) offers a simple survey of the alphabet. Valuable information regarding letter naming and knowledge of words that contain particular initial letters or sounds can be generated through this process. For example, if a child can name all the letters of the alphabet but can only give a corresponding letter-sound for 25% of these and none are vowel sounds, then the teacher knows to target the consonants and vowels the child missed. Jennifer could engage the child in sound games as well as picture and word sorts that emphasize the target letter sounds. Instead of using Clay's survey (2002), Mrs. Berger notes that Jennifer may point to her classroom banner of each letter of the alphabet, which has a picture that illustrates each letter. She would then ask her student to say what the picture is, what the word is, and then what the beginning letter of the word is. Mrs. Berger points out to Jennifer that an informal assessment of the alphabet may also highlight articulation issues. Jennifer administered the assessment to Eric, her 1st grader, and found that he wasn't sure of all his letters (for example, *q* and *y*), and indeed, he had difficulty enunciating the sounds for *s, r,* and *d*.

Concept of Word Assessment

Concept of word assessment involves the understanding that a word can be identified by print surrounded by (white) space and that some words have more than one syllable (Downing & Oliver, 1973; Morris, 1981). Children progress through stages of understanding until a stable concept of a word is established. A useful procedure for assessing progress through these stages is to chorally read a familiar rhyme, such as "Twinkle, Twinkle Little Star," with the child. First, it is chorally read several times with the teacher pointing to each word. Then, the teacher asks the child to read and point independently. Four developmental levels (Eitelgeorge, 2002) can be noted as follows:

- Level 1, not able to match speech to print;
- Level 2, able to match to single-syllable words;
- Level 3, able to match some polysyllabic words, but not all; and
- Level 4, able to match to all words.

Jennifer's student, Eric, scored at a Level 3, but he should be on Level 4, as he is midway through 1st grade.

Concepts of Print Assessment

Concept of print involves collecting information on children's understanding of various text features (words, punctuation and directionality), which is important in developing literacy. Clay's (2002) assessment of the concept of print offers a practical example of assessment in the areas of framing one and two words when asked to, such as recognizing and showing familiarity with the use of punctuation in texts; for instance, with periods, questions, marks and commas. Any picture book can be used. The teacher hands the child the book upside down and backward and asks the child to help her "read" it. Mrs. Berger tells Jennifer to watch how the child orients the book. While going through the book, Jennifer should ask the child to point to a word, to tell her where a period is, where to start (and end) on a page, and so forth. Jennifer found that Eric wasn't sure about some punctuation (commas, quotation marks) and identifying individual words. She realized she was starting to see a pattern in regard to Eric's understanding of the concept of words and looked forward to seeing what she'd learn through the developmental spelling inventory that Mrs. Berger showed her.

Word Knowledge Through Developmental Spelling

Children typically go through common phases in their developmental knowledge of letter-sound associations, patterns in spelling, and word meaning based on derivations. An individual child's developmental spelling knowledge may be ascertained through the use and analysis of a spelling inventory (Bear, Invernizzi, Templeton, & Johnston, 2004). According to Ganske (2000), there are five stages of developmental spelling. The "emergent spelling" stage (prephonetic and semiphonetic) is characterized by scribbles and random letters/numbers, up to the use of individual letters to represent words. In the "letter name" stage, each sound of a word is represented by a letter. The "within word" stage shows awareness of typical spelling patterns when more than one letter is used to represent a sound. At the "syllable juncture" stage, children grow in understanding how syllables work with one another, such as when adding a suffix. Finally, in the "derivational constancy" stage, children's spelling reflects the understanding that roots with shared origins often are spelled the same as well as share meaning.

Analysis of a student's spelling errors can offer vital information to determine a child's developmental understanding of words. For example, if a child can spell single-syllable words with correct beginning and ending consonants, blends, and digraphs, as well as correct short vowels, then he is completing the letter name spelling stage. In addition, if that same student has the aforementioned strengths but displays confusion when using silent-*e* markers for long vowels and confuses medial vowel combinations—for instance, *faed* for *fade, lown* for *loan,* or *crie* for *cry*—then this further confirms that the child is exiting the letter-name stage and moving into the within word stage. Mrs. Berger notes that she often finds that the results correspond to what she learns through the alphabet survey, running records, and writing samples. She also points out that once Jennifer knows the characteristics of the spelling stages, she can easily look at her children's writing instead of administering a developmental spelling inventory. Jennifer found Eric to be in the middle of the letter name stage. He wasn't sure of blends and had difficulty giving each sound a letter.

Anecdotal Record of Receptive and Expressive Vocabulary

Vocabulary is composed of the words a student *receptively* comprehends when listening or reading, as well as the words a student can use *expressively* to communicate in speech and writing. One of the most basic and vital assessment tools is observation, with the recording of that observation through anecdotal records. To support progress, teachers can use whole-group oral discussions; pre-, during-, and post-reading strategies for vocabulary building through guided reading (Fountas & Pinnell, 1996); and written response activities. Jennifer has noted that Eric has an extensive oral vocabulary and is knowledgeable about the world in general.

Mrs. Berger explains that all these assessments for the domain of *conceptual understanding of words* help her identify the child's understandings about words and help her monitor the child's progress. Armed with this knowledge of a child's development, she can then consider the instruction that enhances progress in each area, discussed in the following section.

INSTRUCTION BASED ON ASSESSMENT OF WORD KNOWLEDGE

Since informal assessments can demonstrate a student's understandings along a developmental continuum, it becomes simple for Jennifer to determine the next steps in instruction. She just has to look at the next phase of the continuum. For example, if Jennifer finds her student is mastering the letter name stage of spelling, she can plan her instruction around teaching various vowel digraphs and other elements from the within word stage.

A comprehensive literacy program offers many opportunities to strengthen word understandings in phonemic awareness, alphabetic principle, concept of word, and spelling development. Guided reading, writing workshops, word study through vocabulary study, games, and word sorting provide opportunities for explicit instruction. Jennifer felt confident that she could target the skill areas Eric needed. Still, she wanted more information about his understanding and skill as a reader and writer and so turned to the assessments that Mrs. Berger suggested, which help one see what a child actually does while reading and writing.

ASSESSING THE READING AND WRITING PROCESSES

Reading Development Using a Running Record

A common ongoing reading assessment conducted by teachers today is the running record of students' oral reading (Clay, 2002). A running record provides a written account of a student reading a text. Mrs. Berger tells Jennifer that she tries to get running records from a text on the child's instructional level (i.e., that is read with 90–96% accuracy), because that helps her plan what books to use as she teaches about reading. To take a running record, Mrs. Berger asks the child to read, while she marks on a piece of paper or on a copy of the text exactly what the child says and does. If the child reads a word as written, a check is made; if the child substitutes a word, the substitution is written. The analysis of miscues (miscues are any deviation from the word in print) determines the child's usage of the cueing systems while reading. Mrs. Berger explained that she analyzes how the child uses semantic (meaning), syntactic (language), and graphophonic (visual and phonic) cues. In addition, phrasing, self-correction, use of rereading, and other strategies may be documented. She especially notes whether the child is reading for meaning and is monitoring that what he or she reads makes sense. Using this tool on a regular basis, a teacher can monitor to ensure that the difficulty level of texts read is appropriate, that the student is developing good faculty with strategies, and that progress is occurring.

Looking at Figure 5.2, one can view Eric's running record in January. He read a 1st-grade, Level 6 text (Reading Recovery level) titled *The Seed*. In January one would expect an average 1st-grade reader to be reading at Level 9 or 10. Despite Eric's reading at a level lower than expected, Jennifer could see that Eric had made progress since the beginning of the year. Through analysis of his miscues, she noted some of his strengths and weaknesses. His strengths are in effective use of the semantic and syntactic cueing systems. For example:

> ERIC: "It's not growing too good," said Auntie. "It's not growing," said Billy.
> TEXT: "It's not going to grow," said Auntie. "It's not going to grow," said Bobbie.

Eric's reading makes sense in terms of both language and meaning, but he is less effective in use of the graphophonic cueing system, as shown in the substitution of *growing* for *going* and *good* for *grow*. Jennifer realized that his reading correlates with the results of her other assessments, wherein she identified difficulty in phoneme segmentation through the Yopp–Singer test (Yopp, 1995) and in syllabication in the word-matching assessment (Downing & Oliver, 1973; Morris, 1981). These results also matched with his level of spelling development (Bear et al., 2004), which was at the middle letter name stage. She could see where further direct instruction in word study and prompts to cue him to use graphophonic cues during guided reading would help him gain necessary skills.

FIGURE 5.2. Completed Running Record of *The Seed* for Eric (1st Grade)

√   √   √   √ √ √
Auntie and Bobbie/ planted a seed.//

√   √ √ √ √ √   √
They watered it,/ but it didn't grow.//

√   √ √ √ √ √   √
They raked it,/ but it didn't grow.//

√ √ *growing too good,* √   √
"It's not going to grow,"/ said Auntie.//

√ √ *growing* __ __   √ *Billy 2x, sc*
"It's not going to grow,"/ said Bobbie.//

√   √   √   √   √ √
They went away and forgot it

√   √   √ √   √   √   √ √ √
One day,/ Dad said,/ "Come/ and look at this!//

√   √
A *watermelon!*"

Key:
- The √ means the word was read as it appeared in the text.
- The / represents pauses made by the reader. A short pause is shown by /, while a longer pause is shown by //. Younger readers tend to read by phrases, while more advanced readers tend to read by clauses.
- Words above the text are substitutions made by the reader.
- SC stands for self-correction.
- 2x means the child repeated the word.
- Lines above the text means the child omitted the word.
- Underscore means he placed emphasis on the word.

Reading Fluency

Fluency is the capacity to read texts accurately with syntactical phrasing, appropriate pace, and meaningful expression. To assess fluency, the Zutell and Rasinski (1991) Fluency Scale was adapted to a continuum format by Eitelgeorge and Kent (2001) and is reproduced here with permission of the authors (see Figure 5.3). In this assessment, a student is asked to read a text with which he is familiar (i.e., a second reading) that is also on his instructional level (able to read with 90–96% accuracy). The assessor matches the characteristics of the oral reading with the descriptors on the Oral Fluency Continuum to determine the level of development.

FIGURE 5.3. Oral Reading Fluency

Emerging   *Phrasing*
- Monotonic with little sense of phrase boundaries, word-by-word reading.

Smoothness
- Frequent extended pauses, hesitations, false starts, sound-outs, repetitions and attempts.

Pace
- Slow and laborious.

Developing   *Phrasing*
- Choppy reading with two- and three-word phrases, improper stress and intonation that fails to mark ends of sentences and clauses.

Smoothness
- Several "rough spots" with extended pauses, hesitations that are frequent and disruptive.

Pace
- Moderately slow.

Gaining   *Phrasing*
Fluency
- Fewer run-ons, somewhat choppy with pauses midsentence for breath.
- Reasonable stress and expression.

Smoothness
- Occasional breaks in smoothness caused by difficulties with specific words and structures.

Pace
- Uneven mixture of fast and slow reading.

Fluent   *Phrasing*
- Generally well phrased, mostly in clause and sentence units.
- Good expression.

Smoothness
- Generally smooth reading.
- Some word and structure difficulties that are mostly self-corrected.

Pace
- Consistently conversational.

Note: From Eitelgeorge (2002). Adapted with permission of the author.

In Figure 5.2, Eric is reading *The Seed*. By analyzing his fluency when reading, Jennifer found that Eric has outstanding ability to phrase the text into meaningful units and use expressive intonation and stress. On her running record of Eric's reading, the slash marks demonstrate his phrasing with a partial stop (/) and full stop (//) and an underscore for the word *watermelon* to denote his emphasis and surprise to learn that the seed grew into a watermelon. Using the fluency continuum, Jennifer rated Eric as "developing."

Oral Retelling

Retelling a story as though the teacher had not heard it offers valuable insight into a student's ability to demonstrate how much he or she remembers and comprehends. Retellings occur with different levels of complexity in composition, which reflect a continuum of development (Eitelgeorge, 2002). Setting up a retelling scenario involves two phases. The first phase is an unaided retelling wherein the reader is asked to retell the story without questions from the listener. The second phase is an aided retelling where the teacher assists by posing pertinent questions that provide no new information but lead the child to recall certain parts of the story. In determining what questions to ask, the teacher draws from the story grammar to ask for more information about characters, setting, initiating event, and other factors. Figure 5.4 outlines the levels of complexity of retelling (Eitelgeorge, 2002) as a student progresses through emergent, developing, gaining competency, and competent levels.

The teacher analyzes the retelling for evidence of character, setting, plot episodes, cohesion, and descriptive details. Mrs. Berger explains that it is vital to listen to the child and think about what his or her understanding is. She tells Jennifer to keep in mind that even within the genre of narratives, the story structure can vary, and that each story can have certain parts that are more important than others. Further, children's understanding is affected by their life experiences; success in understanding a story can be attributed to many factors. A role of the teacher is to identify such factors that influence understanding when planning instruction. Using the retelling continuum, Jennifer found Eric to be a "developing" reteller. He needed some prompts, he included most of the elements, but he did not use the same sequence as did the author.

Comprehension Interview

The comprehension interview (Keene & Zimmermann, 1997, see Figure 5.5) taps children's understanding of comprehension-building strategies, including making connections between text and personal experience or other books or knowledge about the world, determining what is important, asking questions, using the senses, making inferences, synthesizing, and solving problems of text. In this assessment, each strategy is given one of four scores to indicate level of understanding. A score of 4 indicates that the child is able to explain how a strategy helps him or her comprehend better. Mrs. Berger informs Jennifer that while the child reads, she targets one or two

FIGURE 5.4. Levels for Retelling

Emerging	• Frequent prompting needed to retell. • First statement often a scanty ending. • Sparse retelling. May include some of the following: major characters, setting, initiating event, no middle, and a terse ending. • Nonsequential retelling. • Sketchy, no details or descriptions.
Developing	• Some prompting needed to retell. • Partial retelling: major characters, setting, beginning, brief middle (events nonsequential), and perhaps an inadequate ending. • Inadequate sequence. • Lacking details and descriptions.
Gaining Competency	• Little prompting needed to retell. • Better-developed retelling: major characters, setting, initiating event, partial middle (cannot lead to a climax), and richer ending. • Developing sequence. • More details and descriptions. • Uses some textual vocabulary. • May extend meaning by linking to personal experience or literature.
Competent	• No prompting needed to retell. • Offers complete retelling: major and minor characters, setting, initiating event, middle with correct sequence (leading to a climax), and end of story or resolution of problem. • Strong sense of sequence. • Rich details and description. • Uses appropriate textual vocabulary. • Shows depth of comprehension by extending meaning, that is, analyzing, critiquing, or linking to other literature and experiences.

metacognitive strategies for interview questions. She is then able to apply the descriptors in the rubric to the child's response. Often, she notes, she does not need to ask questions at all because she has observed the child using the strategies. Eric, Jennifer found, is strong in predicting and is at a Level 2 in most of the other metacognitive strategies (see Figure 5.1).

Writing Development

Writing is a critical area that can be assessed and monitored. The focus is both on the writer's process of narrative writing and on the product. Mrs. Berger is able to track developmental change from compositions that consist of a drawing with labels to ones that hold the basic elements of story grammar

FIGURE 5.5. Comprehension Interview

Strategy	Questions	Rubric	Student Response
Self-Monitors Uses fix-up strategies when meaning breaks down.	What can you do to make the sentence make sense? What else can you do to help you understand?	3) Fix-up strategies help construct meaning. 2) Fix-up strategies do not clear up confusion. 1) No response.	
Connects	What did you think about when you read that part of the story? Did it remind you of something you already knew, or an experience with another book?	3) Response relates background knowledge and personal experiences to text and enhances comprehension. 2) Response is not related to text. 1) No response.	
Summarizes Provides short statements that capture main idea and related details.	What is this part mainly about? Tell me what you just read in one or two sentences.	3) Synthesizes succinctly, recalling main idea and details in sequence. 2) Recalls some events in random order. 1) No response or incorrect.	
Predicts Makes logical predictions based on events.	What do you think will happen next? What might you learn next? What in the text helped you make that prediction?	3) Prediction is consistent and logical with text. 2) Prediction is not substantiated with text. 1) No response.	
Questions Asks questions while reading to clarify meaning or extend understanding.	What did you wonder about as you were reading? What questions did you ask yourself? What confusion did you have?	3) Higher-order question that represents complex thinking about text. 2) Literal question with short answer or word. 1) No response or an unrelated question.	
Infers Reads "between the lines," draws conclusions.	What did the author mean by ___? What made you think of that? What were you thinking when the text said___?	3) Response is logical and shows inferential thinking. 2) Response is literal or not logical. 1) No response.	
Visualizes Creates mental images of characters, events and/or ideas.	What did you picture in your mind? What did the characters look like? What could you draw to illustrate that idea?	3) Image is closely matched with text and further clarifies complex ideas. 2) Image is unrelated to text. 1) No response.	

Note: A score of 4 means the child is able to describe how the strategy aides comprehension.
Adapted from Keene & Zimmerman (1997).

(Eitelgeorge & Barrett, 2004). Mrs. Berger collects writing samples over time as well as observes her children as they write. In addition, she gathers information during the writing conferences about what the writer wants to accomplish. Drawing on these sources, she is able to gain a picture of what the child knows as a writer. She pays attention to what genre the child uses, and she helps the young writer to use the genre effectively. Jennifer looked over the samples of Eric's writing that she had collected since the beginning of the year. She found that he has many ideas, but because he is distracted with spelling and working through sound–symbol correspondence, he loses track of his topic. She decided to talk with him more before he writes and help him complete a simple graphic organizer so that he can remember what he wants to write.

INSTRUCTIONAL RECOMMENDATIONS BASED ON ASSESSMENT OF READING AND WRITING PROCESSES

With the assessment results recorded on the Literacy Assessment Checklist (see Figure 5.1 for Eric's completed checklist), Jennifer can show how she has gathered information about her student's understanding of reading and writing processes.

The running records help Jennifer to assess how her students use syntactic, semantic, and graphophonic systems and how meaning is being made by the reader. To aid growth in any of these three cuing systems, Jennifer can ask questions of the child that prompt him or her to focus on particular cues. For example, she might ask questions suggested by Fountas and Pinnell (1996), such as "Did that make sense? Does it look right? What sound does it start with?" Jennifer can prompt rereading when meaning breaks down. She can also use *think-alouds* to model rethinking about the text.

The retellings become useful to Jennifer not only for comprehension assessment but also as a proven method to enhance comprehension (National Reading Panel, 2000). They allow children to organize thoughts, develop vocabulary, and gain understanding of the grammar (structure) of different genres. Jennifer can guide her students to remember the main elements of genres by their typical story grammar. For example, many narrative stories include characters, settings, problem, plot episodes (attempts toward solution), and a final solution. Jennifer will also teach her students to use a variety of comprehension–building strategies, particularly connection making (text to self, to text, and to world) and use of senses, which work well for 1st graders. She will also help her children learn to synthesize, infer, and ask questions (Keene & Zimmermann, 1997).

Using reading material that is not too difficult but that provides some challenge through which to learn more about the process of reading is critical to any student's instructional program. Jennifer plans to use such books during guided reading with Eric. She knows that if he can read the text well enough, he will be able to think about the strategies and features she is teaching him. She will also make sure that there are plenty of books that Eric can read easily, that is, with an accuracy rate of 97–100%. Mrs. Berger has warned her, however, that although these percentages offer good guidelines, the reader's interest, motivation, and knowledge about a book's content or its characters or the genre can mean that the child is able to understand a book even if he or she has difficulty reading it. Thus, Jennifer wants to have books available based on Eric's interests and knowledge base as well.

Writing provides opportunities to grow in understanding of story grammar, effective expression and communication, and vocabulary knowledge. Further, writing is also a process that helps the child think and, therefore, learn about him- or herself and his or her relationship with the greater sociocultural and natural world. In a literature-rich environment, students will have many models from which to draw for their writing. Instruction should focus on students' writing authentic pieces that have a purpose and audience. In this way, students can develop a strong voice, organizational skills, and rich content, combined with many opportunities for feedback and celebrations of their authoring with peers and the teacher.

CONCLUSION

Using informal literacy assessments, beginning teacher Jennifer is able to compile developmental literacy profiles (see Eric's in Figure 5.1) of her students that will help her make wise instructional decisions. Her goal is to ensure that her students work in their zone of proximal development (Vygotsky, 1978) and continue to progress. Thanks to Mrs. Berger's assistance, Jennifer feels more confident and able to use informal literacy assessments and follow up with instruction that will enhance and support progress.

Teachers have access to many strong research-based assessments that
can keep them informed about their students' progress across the school
year. The ongoing, informal assessments offer immediate feedback. Annual statewide test results often arrive several months after they were administered and are designed to measure children's achievement against
benchmarks. Informal literacy assessments are used to glean data quickly
for each conceptual area and permit the teacher to place the student along
developmental continua. Then, on the basis of these findings, the teacher
selects instructional strategies, observes development, reflects on progress,
and makes necessary modifications. With common instruments teachers
can communicate within and across grade levels to provide more consistent, coherent, and developmental reading and writing instruction for all
students to monitor progress.

PART THREE

Organizing and Using Assessment Data

In this section, the reader is encouraged to take a wider perspective of classroom assessment once again, particularly in reference to how teachers, school leaders, and administrators capitalize on the data generated through action research strategies and the practical strategies a teacher adopts in the classroom. How teachers can involve parents in meaningful classroom assessment processes is also addressed. The section begins by offering valuable technical information that ultimately influences the level of understanding we have about the integrity, validity, and reliability of school and classroom assessments. Throughout this section, an appreciation of the value of collaborative assessment and reflection is in evidence. This appreciation involves the way data is generated and analyzed, as well as an analysis of the assessment practices themselves. Across the different chapters, the value of developing a schoolwide dialogue about the systems of assessment, reflection, and evaluation is highlighted as a valuable process. Breaking possible myths around assessment that parents may hold is encouraged through clear, focused, and simple communication systems—parents can be invited and encouraged to become actively involved in classroom assessment. This is an appropriate ending to the section, as it reminds us that however strong our school and classroom assessments are, it is essential to ensure that we involve all key stakeholders in the process in an informal and welcoming way.

Policy and Technical Considerations for Classroom Assessment

Rosemarie L. Ataya

Andrea Delgado is a new teacher just hired to teach 3rd grade at Sunny-brook Elementary School. She has several ideas for classroom instruction, "but how will I assess my students' knowledge and skills?" She thinks back to her classroom assessment course. "My students will take the state-mandated assessments in math and reading this year, so I should prepare them for the test-item format. I could use some teacher-made tests. What type of items should I create? Should I allow the students to recognize the correct answer in a matching or multiple-choice test? Perhaps the students should recall the information in a fill-in-the-blank test. Tests are not the only way to assess the students. There are also informal observational techniques. I could create a checklist or jot down notes about their behavior. Maybe I can engage the students in a performance task—that way I can observe both the final product and the process. There are so many assessment options to choose from; I'm not quite sure where to begin."

The problem that Andrea confronts is familiar to both novice and veteran teachers. First, a teacher must define *what* to assess. Does Andrea want to know if the students have basic knowledge or if they can apply that knowledge? Once this is decided, a teacher must determine *how* to measure the desired learning outcome. Measurement of learning outcomes occurs through assessment. The type of assessment used depends on the purpose of the assessment as deemed by the teacher or the school administrator. Clearly, any assessment must be of high quality to provide accurate feedback about student learning and teaching effectiveness. Additionally, teachers must adhere to the policy regarding assessment that federal, state, and local governments dictate. Bearing Andrea's situation in mind, my purpose in this chapter is threefold:

- To overview the legislation currently affecting education;
- To describe types of assessment that teachers can use to evaluate teaching; and
- To discuss the technical considerations of various assessment procedures.

CLARIFYING TERMINOLOGY

It is important for teachers to know the differences between measurement, assessment, evaluation, and testing. Many teachers erroneously use these terms interchangeably. *Measurement* is the assignment of numbers to differentiate values of a variable (Kubiszyn & Borich, 2003). For example, if asked to measure the width of this book, a person would take out a ruler and give a numeric value. When teachers measure a student's mathematics achievement, they generate a number to represent that quality. The tool used to generate the mathematics achievement quality is the assessment. *Assessment* consists of all the tools that teachers use to collect information about student learning and instructional effectiveness (Carey, 2001). Many teachers associate assessment with *testing*; however, assessment is broader than testing. In fact, testing is only one component of the assessment process. In a classroom, teachers use tests, presentations, homework, and classwork assignments, as well as observations, to assess student learning. *Evaluation* is the procedure for collecting information and using it to make decisions for which some value is placed on the results (Carey, 2001). For example, when evaluating the success of a high school, one uses standardized-test scores, drop-out and graduation rates, and the number of students who are not promoted.

LEGISLATION AFFECTING ASSESSMENT

Accountability for student education is one of the largest issues in education (Banks, 2005). One of the main goals of accountability systems is the "improvement of instruction and student learning" (Lane, 2004, p. 6). The school accountability movement seeks to evaluate school effectiveness and provide rewards and sanctions based on performance (Smith & Fey, 2000). It dates back to the publication of *A Nation at Risk* (1983) and a widespread belief in an "educational crisis." This legislation was a catalyst for modern education reform. *A Nation at Risk* led to an emphasis on reading, writing, and mathematics instruction in the schools. It also led to competency testing for teachers.

The most recent educational reform is the No Child Left Behind Act of 2001 (NCLB). NCLB, a federal initiative, requires states to implement accountability systems to assess the education of traditionally underserved populations (Wenning, Herdman, Smith, McMahon, & Washington, 2003). This includes

- Students with disabilities;
- Students from major racial and ethnic subgroups;
- Students who are English-language learners; and
- Students who are economically disadvantaged.

The goal of NCLB is to have all students reach the same level of achievement, closing the achievement gap between mainstream students and traditionally underrepresented students (Lane, 2004). States that do not follow NCLB will not receive federal funds for programs.

NCLB requires annual testing in grades 3–8 and in one grade between 10th and 12th in math and reading/language arts by 2006. It also requires testing in science in three grades by 2008. States must also define *basic, proficient,* and *advanced* achievement levels (Linn, Baker, & Betebenner, 2002). The goal is for schools to achieve adequate yearly progress (AYP). AYP requires that a minimum percentage of students in each of the traditionally underserved subgroups attain proficiency. To break down into these subgroups, the size must be "numerically significant," meaning 15% or 100 students at the school site. This is to prevent identification of a single student. For example, if there were only two African American students at a school, breaking down the test scores by race would clearly identify those individual student scores. This requirement of numerically significant prevents that from happening.

In response to No Child Left Behind, almost all states now use standardized achievement tests as the primary or sole mechanism for evaluation (Goertz & Duffy, 2003). Some state systems also include such indicators as attendance, drop-out, graduation, or promotion rates. It is important to note that NCLB requires testing to evaluate the school's performance, not that of individual students. The choice of whether to measure student and teacher accountability rests in the hands of the individual states.

As a result of the federal initiative, many states across the nation have shifted their focus from measuring student learning and thinking to measuring accountability (Lane, 2004). Some of the states have embraced "high-stakes" assessment practices, mainly testing. High-stakes testing is using standardized test scores to determine whether

- Students get promoted to the next grade;
- Students graduate from high school;
- Teachers and administrators receive financial rewards or demotions; and
- School districts receive additional state funds or lose their accreditation.

The push for testing and accountability has stirred debate in the field of education. Individuals and organizations raise questions regarding the place of tests in educational reform (e.g., American Educational Research Association, 2000; Kohn, 2000). Since many states are using standardized tests to assess performance, critics question the characteristics of the tests (e.g., Kohn, 2000; Smith & Fey, 2000). Another issue is the relationship of standardized tests to state standards (Lane, 2004). High-stakes critiques also cite the impact on curriculum and instructional methods (Hilliard, 2000). They accuse policy makers of throwing away high-level thinking skills in favor of rote memorization (e.g., Lane, 2004). Further, this high-stakes atmosphere affects students, increasing their anxiety and worry (Kohn, 2000).

Despite the growing pressures of high-stakes assessment, high-quality teaching can improve student achievement (Hilliard, 2000). Good teaching practices include effectively using assessment. In the following section, I discuss the variety of tools available for teachers to assess student learning and teaching effectiveness.

THE VARIETY OF CLASSROOM ASSESSMENT TOOLS

For assessment to be effective, it is crucial that teachers possess a variety of assessment techniques (Banks, 2005). A teacher who evaluates student learning and instructional practices solely on the basis of test scores is missing valuable information. A test is a snapshot in time, affected by numerous sources of error. There are student factors that can influence a test score, such as the student's being ill on the day of the test. The score earned may not reflect the true knowledge of the topic. The more information a teacher collects, the more valid the inferences based on that information.

There are various types of assessments used in the classroom. As previously mentioned, tests and quizzes constitute one type of tool. These can be teacher-made or adapted from a published source. The alternative to testing is the performance assessment. Performance assessments move away from rote memorization of facts to an application of knowledge and skills (Stiggins, 2005). These assessments are hands-on, requiring students to engage in a complex process or to produce a product (Nitko, 2004). Demonstrations, role-playing and dramatizations, debates, oral presentations, research papers, and experiments are all examples of performance assessment techniques. Performance assessments are not limited to paper-and-pencil or verbal tasks. Nonverbal performance assessments include illustrations, posters, and dioramas.

A growing alternative to testing is the use of portfolio assessments (Popham, 2005). A portfolio is a purposeful collection of student work (Stiggins, 2005). It is not just a folder of work, but rather, work selected to serve a particular purpose (e.g., to document growth or certify achievement). It may contain examples of best work or it may illustrate growth and development.

Other written products, such as journals, are an effective tool to gauge student growth and development (Trice, 2000). Another effective assessment tool is the worksheet, completed at home (homework) or in school (classwork). As with tests and quizzes, teachers can create these worksheets or use those that accompany the classroom textbook. Teachers can embed worksheets into class activities, allowing a continuous instruction-and-assessment process. Cooperative group work, an instructional technique, can also serve as an assessment technique (Trice, 2000). Even personal communication between a teacher and student can serve as a form of assessment (Stiggins, 2005). The merge of instructional and assessment activities is referred to as *embedded assessment* (Wilson & Sloan, 2000).

An embedded assessment technique frequently used in classrooms is observational assessment. An observation, whereby a teacher watches what students say or do, is an effective assessment tool. Teachers can record the observation as written notes or summaries of behavior, a tally of frequencies based on a checklist, or measures on a rating scale indicating a degree of change (Gonzalez, Brusca-Vega, & Yawkey, 1997). Teachers can create their own checklists and rating scales or use published instruments.

There are also alternate assessment processes for students with identified special educational needs. The terms *alternate* and *alternative* when applied to assessments are often used interchangeably, but in reality these are very different. Alternate assessments are assessment processes specifically intended for students who are following alternate curriculum standards. Such alternate assessments are intended to monitor progress and measure adequate yearly progress of this group of learners. The alternate assessment process is variable across the nation, with differences occurring not only across states, but also between districts in each of the states. There is currently some positive movement toward a cohesive understanding of alternate assessments and new practices are being seen (Browder, Flowers, Ahlgrim-Delzell, Karvonen, Spooner, & Algozzine, 2004). Alternate assessment procedures may include criterion-referenced assessments, portfolios, informal student work, and structured teacher observations.

The previous paragraphs make clear the diversity of classroom assessments available to teachers. Assessments can be categorized along several dimensions. In the following section, I discuss the multidimensional nature of assessment.

THE MULTIPLE DIMENSIONS OF CLASSROOM ASSESSMENT

Assessment is multidimensional, consisting of several different categories (Banks, 2005). Assessments are categorized on the basis of the method of development (teacher-made versus standardized), the nature of the task (traditional versus alternative), the instructional purpose (formative versus summative), the level of formality (formal versus informal), the grading standard (criterion referenced versus norm referenced), the type of item format (selected response versus constructed response), and the type of scoring procedure (objective versus subjective). In exploring these multidimensional characteristics, Andrea, the new teacher in the vignette at the beginning of this chapter, will be in a much stronger position to make some key assessment decisions.

Teacher-Made Versus Standardized Assessments

The classroom teacher creates a teacher-made assessment for a specific instructional purpose. For example, if Andrea wants to know if her students can apply writing conventions (i.e., correctly uses capitalization), she can create a worksheet designed to assess that skill. Typically, teacher-made assessments lack formal validity and reliability information because of variability in the classroom procedures. Andrea's writing assessment may differ considerably from that of her colleague in the adjacent 3rd-grade classroom. To make comparisons with other 3rd-grade students, Andrea should use a standardized assessment.

People with specialized knowledge and training in test construction design standardized assessments. The process of standardization refers to the assessment and scoring procedures. Every person who takes the assessment responds to the same items under the same conditions. The answers are evaluated according to the same scoring standards. The scores are interpreted through comparison to the scores obtained from a group that took the same assessment under the same conditions or through comparison with a predetermined standard. The purpose of a standardized assessment is to obtain an accurate and representative sample of some aspect of a person (e.g., writing achievement, behavioral improvement). This allows the teacher to identify strengths and weaknesses, plan instruction, and select students for programs. Andrea may use a standardized test such as the Test of Written Language (TOWL-3) to assess writing conventions and use the results to identify students for remediation. She may also use the results to compare her students to other 3rd-grade students who took the assessment.

Alternative Versus Conventional (Traditional) Assessments

Alternative assessments refer to any assessment that is not a test (Nitko, 2004). Performance assessments (such as demonstrations and projects) and portfolio assessments are both forms of alternative assessment. Many educators use the term *authentic assessment* to describe these alternative assessments. Some assessment specialists question the existence of truly authentic assessments (Hambleton, 1996). For purposes of this discussion, authentic assessments emphasize realistic performance measures, where students are actively engaging in a behavior (Banks, 2005).

Formative Versus Summative Assessments

When using assessments, teachers need to decide if they will be evaluating the students' overall product or the process during the product's creation. If they decide to evaluate the process or procedure involved in the assessment, they are engaging in formative assessment. Formative assessment is an ongoing process that includes giving feedback and direction to students as they proceed toward a goal. Formative assessment is important when correct procedure is crucial to later success, when analysis of procedural steps can aid in improving the final product, and when learning is at an early stage (McMillan, 2004). It is a primary component of assessment for learning (Black, Harrison, Lee, Marshall, & Wiliam, 2003). For example, if Andrea wants to monitor her students' writing progress, she can have her students write multiple drafts of a story. She can provide feedback on the multiple components involved in writing and track individual student growth. Formative assessment is also effective for improving instruction. Andrea may find that several of her students are having difficulty with grammar and syntax. This allows her to provide remediation for the students who need extra help. Formative assessment techniques include conversations with students, class discussions, questioning during instruction, daily homework and classwork, teacher-made quizzes and tests, and student portfolios (Nitka, 2004).

If teachers decide to evaluate the final product, they are engaging in summative assessment. Summative assessment documents student learning at the end of a unit of study, measuring learning outcomes. Going back to our example, Andrea may decide to grade the final draft of the story that illustrates her students' ability to incorporate all aspects of the writing process.

Formal Versus Informal Assessments

Formal assessments are those assessments that are planned and structured (Banks, 2005). Typically, formal assessments assist teachers in making judgments about student knowledge. The goal is differentiating between those who know the information and those that do not (Banks, 2005). These assessments include quizzes, tests, performance assessments, and portfolio assessments. For example, Andrea might assess her students' reading comprehension through a test where the students read a passage and answer questions about the passage regarding the main idea and key events. In addition, Andrea may decide to use personal communication with her students as an indicator of comprehension. She may pose questions orally to the students to gauge their understanding of the passage. This is an informal assessment technique. Informal assessments allow teachers to identify the students' level of development and guide instruction. It also allows teachers to observe the variability in individual student learning (Banks, 2005). Typically, informal assessments are not graded (Nitko, 2004). Informal techniques include teacher observations, anecdotal records, and personal communication with the students.

Criterion-Referenced Versus Norm-Referenced Assessments

Criterion-referenced assessments involve comparing a student's performance with an objectively stated standard of achievement (Kubiszyn & Borich, 2003). It indicates how much knowledge was learned. It also indicates the degree of mastery of skills that have been taught. Criterion-referenced assessments may be used to determine how well a student is learning. They may also be used to determine how well the teacher is teaching the curriculum. Content for a criterion-referenced assessment is selected on the basis of curriculum and learning objectives. When Andrea wants to gauge student learning, she will give an assessment that measures her instructional objectives. Student performance is evaluated with reference to Andrea's instructional objectives.

Norm-referenced assessments compare one student with another (Kubiszyn & Borich, 2003). They are designed to rank-order students. Norm-referenced assessments help schools classify students into special education or gifted programs. They also help teachers select students for different ability-level instructional groups. Content for a norm-referenced assessment is selected on how well it ranks students. If Andrea wants to place her students into reading groups, she may give an assessment that contains broad reading skills. The students who score at the bottom will receive increased instruction on basic reading skills. Since Andrea is ranking her students, this reflects a norm-referenced assessment.

Selected-Response Versus Constructed-Response Assessments

Selected-response assessments require the student to select the answer from a list of alternatives (McMillan, 2004). Test and quiz items typically fall into this category. These include matching, true/false, and multiple-choice items. Going back to our vignette, Andrea may decide to assess student ability to select the main idea from a series of short stories. She could pose the questions as multiple-choice items and allow the students to choose from among the responses. This would allow Andrea to assess her students' ability to select the main idea from a story.

Constructed-response assessments require the student to supply rather than select the correct answer. It is a measure of recall rather than recognition (McMillan, 2004). Fill-in-the-blank, short-answer, and essay test items fall into this category. Andrea may decide to measure her students' knowledge of the main idea in a story by having them read a book of their choice and identify the main idea.

Objective Versus Subjective Assessments

When only one correct answer exists, it is an objective assessment. These responses are either correct or incorrect without the need for interpretation. Although typically linked with tests, performance assessments can be scored objectively. For example, Andrea's students conduct an experiment to determine if a person would float better in salt water or in tap water. Andrea may have a list of procedures that the students must correctly follow. Either the students followed the procedures for the lab experiment or they did not.

Subjective assessments allow for multiple answers to a problem. This allows for student creativity and encourages thinking outside the box. Andrea may allow her students to test various materials for their buoyancy in both tap and salt water. Students may select different materials. Allowing for multiple answers is not the same as lacking a clear scoring procedure. Unclear scoring procedures jeopardize the technical quality of an assessment (Nitko, 2004; Popham, 2005).

TECHNICAL CONSIDERATIONS IN ASSESSMENT

Although traditionally affiliated with testing, the concepts of validity, reliability, and absence of bias are critical when using any form of assessment. In this section I will discuss the elements of designing valid and reliable tools that are free from bias.

In general, the higher the stakes, the greater the demand for formal measures of validity, reliability, and balance. For example, a statewide assessment or an exam that must be passed for graduation would require extensive, formal technical review, while a classroom-level formative performance assessment may not. Nevertheless, it is important for the classroom teacher to consider technical issues, even if informally, because technical quality helps determine confidence in the assessment and its results.

Validity

Validity asks the question, Does the assessment measure what it is supposed to? The term *validity* is frequently used when discussing tests but it is a crucial element in any type of assessment. Going back to our vignette, perhaps Andrea decides to use a book report to measure her students' knowledge of the book *Mr. Popper's Penguins*. She will assess her students' ability to identify the main idea of the story, character development, and the events that occur in the story. Andrea may be looking for other elements as well. Are the students able to write paragraphs? Can the students organize information? The decision to assess the students with a book report rather than a test indicates that Andrea wants her students to do more than recite information.

In instruction, teachers decide what to teach, selecting what is pertinent from a large curriculum and state standards. Assessment requires the same behavior. Teachers not only ask, "What will I assess," they also need to determine the most effective way to assess it. The key to accomplishing this task is having clearly measurable instructional objectives. Additionally, these objectives must be appropriate to the selected assessment. For example, if a teacher has her students orally recite a poem, one would expect that the students' oral speaking ability is one objective. If it is not part of the instructional objectives, then it should not be part of the assessment. Matching instructional objectives to the assessment is the hallmark of *content validity* (Popham, 2005).

When creating tests or quizzes, teachers should use a blueprint or a table of specifications to align instructional objectives to the actual test content (Kubiszyn & Borich, 2003). The test blueprint is a two-way table that gives a basic design for a test. Figure 6.1 illustrates a test blueprint for a 10-item 2nd-grade social studies quiz. The horizontal axis of the test blueprint gives an outline of the content to be covered in terms of instructional objectives. The vertical axis lists the cognitive levels that are the target of instruction. The cells indicate the number of test items representing each instructional objective and the cognitive level. The number of test items representing a specific objective should match the amount of time of instruction. For example, in Figure 6.1, 4 out of 10 items on the social studies quiz measure a student's ability to locate places on a map of the United States. Therefore, 40% of the class instruction should reflect this objective.

A second aspect of content validity is related to the accuracy of the content. States and other large-scale assessment developers have assessments reviewed by content experts—economists, mathematicians, poets, and so forth—to ensure that the content presented is correct. Even though it is not practical for a classroom teacher to engage academics for this purpose, teachers may provide quick content checks for one another on a regular basis.

When selecting a published test, it is imperative that the test be used for its intended purpose (American Educational Research Association, American Psychological Association, & National Council on Measurement in Education, 1999). For example, if Andrea wants to identify students who have reading difficulties, she should use a test that is diagnostic. In addition, teachers should match the content of the test to their instructional objectives.

FIGURE 6.1. Sample Test Blueprint for 2nd–Grade Social Studies Quiz

Instructional Objectives	Knowledge Level	Comprehension Level	Total Number of Items	Percentage of Test	Item Number
The student can match famous people that held/hold offices with their positions.	4		4	40%	1 – 4
The student can make predictions based on information given in bar graphs.		2	2	20%	5 – 6
The student can locate significant places discussed in class on a map of the United States.	4		4	40%	7 – 10
Total	8	2	10	100%	

Matching instructional objectives to the assessment is also imperative when using performance assessments (Nitko, 2004). For example, if Andrea assigns a travel brochure as an assessment, the objectives must match the required elements of the project and the skills necessary to complete the task. If the students are required to research the country and report on certain elements, ability to find information (researching) should be one of her objectives.

The instructional objectives should also match the scoring rubric. Rubrics provide a common basis for judging all students and ensure that standards are less likely to shift during grading. Having a well-developed rubric enhances reliability, validity, and fairness of scoring. The scoring rubric used should depend on the teacher's purpose. There are two types of scoring rubrics: analytical and holistic. Analytical rubrics focus on multiple dimensions of performance and giving feedback. Holistic rubrics focus on overall understanding rather than on individual skills. These rubrics provide a single overall score with no separate dimensions. This type of rubric provides less feedback to students about strengths and weaknesses. Figure 6.2 illustrates an analytical rubric and Figure 6.3 illustrates a holistic rubric.

Informal assessments are often criticized in terms of validity (Banks, 2005). Observational assessments can be prone to subjectivity if the behaviors are not clearly defined. Therefore, when using observational checklists and rating scales, a teacher should define the terms to minimize broad interpretations (Gonzalez, Brusca–Vega, & Yawkey, 1997). In addition, teachers should not infer meaning when writing anecdotal records. Instead, they

FIGURE 6.2. Sample Analytic Scoring Rubric

	Score		
Criteria	0	1	2
Creativity	Student does not use any original ideas to make his or her points.	Student uses his or her imagination to create one or two new ideas.	Student uses his or her imagination to create at least three new ideas.
Knowledge	Student does not recall any events discussed in class.	Student recalls one or two events discussed in class.	Student recalls at least three events discussed in class.
Relevance	Fewer than half of the points made are relevant to the question being asked.	Half of the points made are relevant to the question being asked.	Most of the points made are relevant to the question being asked.

FIGURE 6.3. Sample Holistic Scoring Rubric

Score	Criteria
5	Accurately provides all 10 pieces of information requested from the lesson (3 specific descriptors, 1 benefit, and 1 disadvantage for each type of bankruptcy). The comparison will state how each type of bankruptcy affects a consumer's credit rating. Is legible and well written, and there is no extraneous information. There are no errors in syntax or grammar.
4	Accurately provides 7–9 pieces of information requested from the lesson. The comparison will state the benefits and disadvantages of each type of bankruptcy. Is legible and well written, and there is no extraneous information. There are no errors in syntax or grammar.
3	Accurately provides 5–6 pieces of information requested from the lesson. The comparison will state a benefit and/or disadvantage of one or both types of bankruptcy. Is legible and well written, but possesses some extraneous information. There are some errors in syntax and grammar.
2	Accurately provides 3–4 pieces of information requested from the lesson. No comparison is made of the two types of bankruptcy. Is legible but poorly written, and possesses some extraneous information. There are many errors in syntax and grammar.
1	Accurately provides 1–2 pieces of information requested from the lesson. No comparison is made of the two types of bankruptcy. Is illegible and poorly written and possesses much extraneous information. There are many errors in syntax and grammar.
0	Does not provide any of the requested information or does not attempt to answer question.

should write straightforward descriptions of what happened and what students say. The same recommendation holds true for personal communications with students. Accurate records are necessary to ensure validity of the discussion (Stiggins, 2005).

Another type of validity is *decision validity*—the degree to which decisions based on assessments are defensible. In the classroom these decisions might include, for example, placement or grouping assignments (based on diagnostic assessment), instructional decisions (based on formative assessment), and grading decisions (based on summative assessment).

To increase decision validity, the classroom teacher should consider multiple measures, each based on common standards or objectives, and all aligned with expected levels of student performance. Again, the level of time and effort necessary for decision validity is determined largely by whether the decision is high stakes for the student.

Reliability

While validity is concerned with the accuracy of an assessment, reliability focuses on the consistency of scores. Many forms of reliability pertain mainly to formal assessment techniques (e.g., tests). These include test-retest reliability and alternate-forms reliability. Test-retest reliability indicates stability over time. This type is most appropriate when evaluating a test designed to measure something assumed to be relatively stable over time. This form of reliability is computed by administering the same test twice to the same group with a time interval between administrations. For example, IQ is believed to be a stable trait. If a person completed an IQ test at 7 years old and retakes it today, the score will be in the same range. This illustrates the test-retest reliability. If, however, a teacher is using a pretest and gives an intervention to improve learning, the reliability will be low upon completing the posttest. Therefore, test–retest reliability is not appropriate for a pretest–posttest situation.

Alternate-form reliability is also known as parallel-forms or equivalence reliability. In this form of reliability, two forms of a test (measuring same constructs but with different items) are given to the same group with little or no intervening time interval. Let's say that Andrea is teaching two sections of a math class, one in the morning and the other in the afternoon. She might not want to give the same exam to both classes for fear that the items may be compromised. Instead, she creates two versions of the test (measuring similar content). If Andrea pilot-tests it with one of the classes, she would expect the scores on both versions of the test to be equivalent. This is evidence of alternate-form reliability.

Several assessments are affected by a third form of reliability: interrater. Interrater reliability represents the degree of agreement (consistency) between two or more scorers. This is typically represented by percentage agreement. Despite valid scoring rubrics and clear descriptors of behavior, common rating errors do occur. One type is personal-bias errors. These occur where the observer or rater did not use the whole rating scale. This results in a *generosity error*, where the student is rated favorably on all aspects; a *central tendency error*, where the student is rated in the middle; or the *severity error*, where the student is rated low on all aspects of the rating form. The problem with this is that the scores may reflect the rater as much as the student. There is also little variability in the scores.

Another type of rating error is the halo effect, where initial ratings influence subsequent ratings. A general impression colors all achievement ratings for a student. For example, if Andrea rates the behavior positively on the first observation, then in future assessments she will rate the student positively regardless of the actual behavior. The problem with this is that it obscures students' strengths and weaknesses. It is also a form of prejudice. This typically happens when teachers grade written products by their students (Trice, 2000). To prevent this error, grade student responses anonymously (Kubiszyn & Borich, 2003).

Interrater reliability can be enhanced dramatically through the process of *calibration*. The calibration process typically involves the following steps:

- Determining performance descriptors clearly explaining the type and level of work expected;
- Identifying student work that is representative of each performance level;
- Training teachers in the performance levels;
- Assessing exemplars and sharing ratings and rationale; and
- Measuring levels of reliability, then repeating this process.

Not only can calibration dramatically increase interrater reliability, it is also an exceptional professional development activity, as it is grounded in student work, involves teacher engagement in collaborative learning, and has direct application to the classroom. The process is especially valuable when common classroom assessments, such as rubrics, are used commonly across classrooms.

Fairness and Bias

While the terms *fairness* and *bias* are often used interchangeably, they have different meanings as related to technical considerations for assessment. *Fairness* is a broad term that includes bias and other aspects of the use of assessments. Fairness be may related to an opportunity to learn. Has the student had the chance to learn what is expected? For example, if a student is given a performance test related to using a computer, has computer access and instruction occurred in the classroom? Fairness may also relate to opportunity to perform. Does the assessment give the student the chance to show what he or she knows or can do? Providing opportunity to perform may require accommodations, modifications, or alternate assessment opportunities. Beyond opportunity, fairness includes fairness of use. Do students know what the purpose of the assessment is? Do they know how results will be used? Are conclusions reached about the assessment and decisions made on the basis of it valid?

Bias gives an advantage to certain individuals or groups. For example, an assessment that bases a writing prompt on extensive prior knowledge of baseball may be biased against students whose culture or lifestyle do not relate to that sport. Common forms of assessment bias relate to gender, language, culture, race, ethnicity, and economic status. Classroom assessments are useful only to the degree that the teacher is confident in the information they provide and the degree to which he or she can rely on the results. While the need for technical rigor varies depending on the potential impact on students, a working knowledge of validity, reliability, fairness, and bias is an essential asset in the classroom.

Action Research and Classroom Assessment

Elizabeth Larkin and Sharon Miller Keller

Nina arrived at the first meeting of the action research group with six of her colleagues. As part of a Professional Development School (PDS) initiative, the group was convened by a university professor (Larkin) not for a formal course to be taught, but for a shared opportunity to explore problems of practice and plan action research projects focused on classroom assessment for improving student learning. The first hour's discussion mainly addressed how the participants wanted to organize the sessions and what their time commitment would be. Time was the major challenge, which ultimately caused the group to dwindle down to just three classroom teachers. Upon leaving, one participant said, "I thought we were just going to journal. You're saying we're supposed to design a research project. I don't have that kind of time." In the end, three of the original participants chose to leave. The three who remained had pressing issues they wished to address, despite the time it would take. The opportunity to do action research offered them a concrete pathway toward answering their own questions, and they were eager to get started. They began by setting up future meetings.

Action research is a powerful strategy for reexamining the uses of assessment and a valid tool for changing teaching practices because it is self-motivated and driven by a personal need to know. Teachers develop both positive and negative assumptions about assessment from years of personal experience, first as learners and then as instructional leaders. Today's classrooms demand a shift in thinking that redefines the purposes of assessment as informing not only student learning but also instructional choices: "Professional development situated in the work of teachers is considered critical for classroom improvements that lead to increased student achievement" (McMunn, McColskey, & Butler, 2004, p. 3). Engaging in action research can help teachers become more invested in solving their own problems of practice and more collaborative in interpreting assessment data and making decisions about needed changes. In addition, action research can serve to complement top-down mandates and high-stakes testing so that teachers can confidently select the most effective instructional strategies.

This chapter will follow a case study of a teacher, Nina, who continued to seek professional development opportunities that were meaningful learning experiences for her as well as valuable vehicles for helping the students she taught. The vignettes will show each step in planning and executing an action research project. The teacher in this story had tried numerous strategies to support her students' learning, but she still felt puzzled by the lack of discernable progress. So, despite being immersed in a busy professional and personal life, she volunteered to participate in an action research initiative in order to make better-informed instructional choices and demonstrate how she was making a difference in the lives of struggling middle school learners in an affluent suburban community.

DEFINING ACTION RESEARCH

Action research is a strategy to go beyond personal intuition about individual students by collecting evidence in a systematic way that shows how they learn best. At first, this might appear daunting and too time consuming for classroom practitioners. Nina commented that she decided to commit the time because "as teachers we continue to do things the same way. Maybe we should do things differently and get out of our comfort zone and look at whether we are as effective as we think we are." An impetus for change that emerges from within and is based on compelling evidence will not be resisted by teachers in the way it would be if it were a reform mandate.

> Classroom Action Research (CAR) is a systematic inquiry with the goal of informing practice in a particular situation. CAR is a way for instructors to discover what works best in their own classroom situation, thus allowing informed decisions about teaching. . . . CAR occupies a midpoint on a continuum ranging from teacher reflection at one end to traditional educational research at the other. It is more data-based and systematic than reflection, but less formal and controlled than traditional educational research. (Mettetal, 2002–2003, p. 1)

A pioneer of action research, Stephen Corey (1953), points out that action and research occur in an ongoing cycle of inquiry:

> Action research . . . is a practice in which no distinction is made between the practice being researched and the process of researching it. Teaching is not one activity and inquiring into it another. The ultimate aim of inquiry is understanding, and understanding is the basis for improvement. (p. 3)

Using action research as a tool shifts assessment away from being only an external evaluation of effectiveness toward being one that is integral to teacher choice and voice in the professional growth process. Action research can be useful in deciding how to set up the classroom environment, in knowing which curriculum models to select, and in finding out how to identify preferred instructional and evaluation strategies. Used as a routine strategy, it allows teachers to consider the consequences of their decisions in everyday practice. The excitement of getting results that inform decisions can be catching, and once teachers are hooked, the issue of finding time to participate in action research projects begins to diminish. When a culture of inquiry pervades daily practice, action research no longer seems like an add-on. Having the forum for dialogue encourages the change process that is essential to improving professional practice.

Using action research as a tool to investigate classroom assessment practices is a cycle that begins with recognizing a problem to be solved or a question that demands data to answer. Figure 7.1 shows the steps in the process.

FIGURE 7.1. The Action Research Cycle

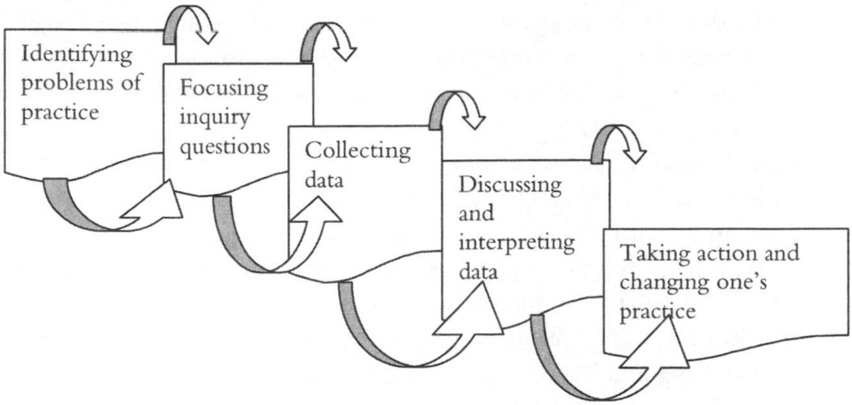

The action research process is a looping cycle that continues at increasingly complex levels to improve pedagogy and student performance (Berg, 2001). Recognizing the need for better information about student learning, effective teaching, and classroom assessment, teachers are turning to action research strategies as a supplement to the quantitative measures of standardized testing.

IDENTIFYING PROBLEMS OF PRACTICE

At the second meeting, Nina and her colleagues brainstormed possible topics for their action research projects. There were lots of ideas tossed around and many problems of practice identified, but the specific question to pursue was elusive. Nina thought she might look into reasons for low achievement among several of her classes, so she left this session thinking about the specific focus her study might take.

The steps outlined in Figure 7.1 offer a process to examine assessment practices in the context of classroom teaching. As Bullough and Gitlin (1995) point out, it is "[your] concerns as they emerge in the classroom that are the focus of your study" (p. 181). Improving teaching, learning, and assessment in the classroom may include looking closely at individual students, inquiring into curriculum design, or examining the effectiveness of particular pedagogical and assessment approaches. It begins with a question or puzzle that cannot be answered by simply reading a text or asking for advice.

The brainstorming session was a vehicle for generating a list of common problems shared by others, so that Nina did not have to feel alone in her struggle to identify a topic worthy of methodical investigation. The collaborative conversation sparked ideas that she could then consider further during the intervening weeks until the group met again. To help her thinking, Nina talked with other teachers and read some articles about motivating low-achieving students.

Sagor (2005) recommends using reflective writing as a process to find the initial focus of a research study. The experience of writing freely in a journal and then reflecting on feelings that emerge (e.g., frustrations, curiosities, surprises, satisfactions) can help busy teachers zero in on questions that really matter in relation to the assessment practices they use in their classrooms. When teachers keep a journal to track the development of their thinking and learning about a topic such as classroom assessment, they typically are able to identify and name the problems, issues, and questions that plague their practice.

FOCUSING INQUIRY QUESTIONS

The school's principal stopped by to lend her support to the action re-search initiative, and to let the teachers know that she had a research question she hoped someone would investigate: "Will more genuinely earned recognition decrease the achievement gap and improve student performance and attitude?" She was planning to institute a new school-wide system of awards to motivate the lowest-achieving students who could never be successful under the current system that only recognized the highest levels of achievement. She wanted to support students with low achievement by recognizing any improvement, and she needed data to show whether the new program made a difference. Nina, who taught students with identified special needs, from gifted to learning disabled, decided to take the challenge.

Questioning what one does as an educator, why one holds his or her beliefs, and how one can accomplish his or her goals is the mark of a "reflective practitioner" (Schön, 1987). Pursuing research questions often leads to more questions that beg investigation, as in the magician's trick of pulling out one scarf, another, then another, and yet another. Narrowing the research focus can be challenging, and this first step in the process can be facilitated by both collaborative conversation (through creating an action research group) and time for individual reflection. In Nina's case, the principal's goals resonated with her own curiosity about the effectiveness of using rewards. As a result, Nina began to consider specific low-achieving students she thought she could help if she knew more about how assessments could be used to motivate them.

The development of questions worthy of action research is often an ongoing exploration of personal ideology, and then developing an understanding of a problem together with others in the shared context of the particular school culture. The process of generating and exploring potential questions is best done in conversation with others, because it brings together multiple perspectives, and the dialogue eventually sharpens thinking into clearer questions that can be investigated realistically in the classroom. Critical questioning about student learning and what learning involves, along with examination of the literature on assessment, leads to planning systematic steps to reconsider, restate, and reposition ideas about assessment. Exploring different perspectives should include not only talking with colleagues in the current practical context, but also finding out about the applications and relevance of the problem being investigated to outside educational settings.

According to Mettetal (2002–2003, p. 1), a good question has three essential characteristics:

1. It is significant to the particular classroom situation.
2. It is likely to lead to a change in practice.
3. It leads to research that "is feasible in terms of time, effort, and resources."

An example of well-defined, guiding questions can be seen in a study documenting a classroom teacher's investigation of incorporating multiple assessments in a grade 9 applied mathematics class (Lim & Colgan, 2005). The inquiry questions were, What are the factors that impede or facilitate the implementation of multiple assessments? and What are the students' views of being assessed through multiple assessments?

Sometimes it can be useful to formulate open-ended "frames" to stimulate the development of more-specific questions for action research about classroom assessment. Here are some examples:

- Do students learn more skills when engaged in assessing their own writing?
- How do other teachers provide feedback to students after using rubrics to assess science investigations?
- How do other teachers modify their assessments after mandated changes are made to the curriculum?
- How can my use of portfolio assessments take less time?

COLLECTING DATA

Nina's initial step in pursuing the research question posed by the principal was to get student-progress data from the first quarter as a baseline. Next, she decided to focus her attention only on the 6th graders, the youngest class in middle school, because they were just learning the school culture. The first time that they could receive recognition would not be until after the first quarter.

Nina compared student GPAs from the beginning of the school year through each quarter to see if scores were improving or declining. She tracked which students received straight A's (4.0), honors (3.5–3.9), honorable mention (3.0–3.4), or had 100% "employability" (determined by attendance, homework, and other indicators that contributed 20% of the grade) in the first quarter and compared those GPAs with second- and third-quarter scores. Between the second and third quarters, she had parent conferences with some students who were not achieving as expected and she verbally praised other students in front of their peers for improving their scores. Preliminary results indicated that students who were publicly recognized in the Awards Assembly tended not to improve, and students whose parents demonstrated that they cared about their children's achievement did show improvement.

In action research, data collection is a cumulative process in which additional collection methods may be added along the way. Then, all sources of evidence are "triangulated" (cross-referenced) to check for consistent themes or indicators. Typically, data-collection strategies include the following:

- *Systematic observation.* Observation using a checklist or a template of particular items or writing rich, descriptive notes to document what is happening can be unobtrusive and provide a wealth of useful data. Additional descriptive notes can be added later to flesh out details and nuances. Systematic looking requires making some decisions about when to observe, how often, and for how long in order to capture good information.
- *Document analysis.* Looking at a collection of existing artifacts, such as examples of student work, samples of student assessments, parent conference reports, and so forth, can shed light on progress over time. Comparing work samples from early in the school year to what the student is currently doing should show clear patterns of change.
- *Interviews.* Structured interviews involve asking the same set of questions of a group or a representative sample for comparison. Semistructured interviews follow the same set of questions, but allow for probing digressions to clarify ideas. Focus groups often use an unstructured format that begins with a topic or overarching question, and further questions emerge out of the participants' interaction. Action researchers use interviews to gain insight into the perspectives of colleagues, students, family members, and school and district administrators.
- *Surveys.* Surveys are relatively quick to administer and analyze, particularly if done online, and they can include questions for which respondents use a scale to answer (e.g., 1–5, from "agree strongly" to "disagree strongly") or respondents can write short answers to open-ended questions. It is essential to limit the length and number of surveys any particular group is asked to complete in order to get a high rate of response. Surveys are useful for generating information about wide-ranging or popular trends.

In general, as is the case in all good classroom assessment, it is essential to use multiple measures, using either more than one type of data-collection strategy or the same method more than once. Doing so helps to build confidence in the results because they can be confirmed when cross-referenced. Also, it is wise to field-test any survey instruments to ensure that they are clear and will produce the desired information. Field tests can be conducted with a small number of individuals, trying out the survey with just two colleagues, for example, before sending it out to the entire sample of respondents. Adjustments can then be made before data are collected and interpretation begins.

DISCUSSING AND INTERPRETING DATA

Nina was more perplexed about her professional practice as a result of her action research than she had been at the outset of her project, because she had expected to see that praising students would encourage them to improve. Although Nina had read Alfie Kohn's book *Punished by Rewards* (1993), she was still surprised to see evidence that rewarding the students was in fact counterproductive. She realized that other variables could have created the drop in scores, so she was motivated to investigate this question further. She wondered what grade level was most appropriate for beginning to move toward a more internal locus of control for achievement. What interventions could be tried next? She needed the ongoing dialogue with her peers not only to plan additional steps in her research, but also to present an argument to the principal for changing the new system of rewards schoolwide if the evidence consistently demonstrated that this strategy wasn't working.

Interpreting data is the most exciting part of action research when results begin to take form. Again, the steps in the analysis process must proceed systematically to guard against jumping to conclusions prematurely. Looking for patterns and trends in the data requires being thoroughly familiar with everything, so the first step is to sift through all the sources that have been collected more than once. After immersion in the data, themes emerge and categories can be identified for sorting the information (a process called *coding* that remains fluid for a while). Drawing from the multiple sources helps to develop the themes and trends that have been initially identified. The different sources are then used to cross-reference (triangulate) the data to confirm or disconfirm the evolving patterns in each coding category. Once the data have been organized into clear categories, it is easier to see the repeating themes and confirming evidence. Sorting the data can be done manually (cutting and pasting documents) or by using technology (various software programs are available).

Interpreting collected data involves gathering relevant information from published sources as well as drawing upon observations (insightful comments within field notes), reflective journal notes, and interactive dialogue with colleagues. Typically, prompting questions such as the following are asked in the interpretation phase: "How does the information collected surprise you? What confirming evidence supports a new understanding about the topic? What challenges do these understandings pose in the classroom context? What other variables could account for the results? What new questions now need to be answered?"

An example of how the interpretation stage of a research project can have a widespread positive effect on assessment practices can be found in the action research study of Brookhart, Andolina, Zuza, and Furman (2004). In this project, 3rd-grade students reflected each week on their work in problem solving and their successes in learning. The analysis of student self-assessments led teachers to successfully turn the rote-memorization task of learning the times tables into a more meaningful experience for the students.

A critical aspect of teachers' conducting participatory action research (Bogdan & Biklen, 2003) is that the project design, data analysis, and interpretation steps include collaboration. Working together provides safeguards against personal biases and subjectivity in a process of reflection about teaching effectiveness. Working together also creates support for collecting data systematically and within a given time frame.

Conditions that invite teachers to use action research in a collaborative way as a means of changing their classroom assessment practices include the following:

- Time and space for colleagues to meet;
- Administrative acknowledgment of the value of action research and its relationship to improving teaching, learning, and assessment;
- Access to expertise to guide research design;
- Resources to collect and analyze data;
- Reflective dialogue among peers who are interested in improving professional practice;
- Multiple opportunities to experiment, think, and write;
- A forum to share recommendations for future practice; and
- The power to establish personal voice and choice within the daily experience of teaching and professional development with hopes of shaping school policy.

TAKING ACTION AND CHANGING ONE'S PRACTICE

Nina planned to document systematically the recognition interventions that occurred between the third- and fourth-quarter scores. She would also interview other teachers of these 6th-grade students to ask about the difficulty of the subject matter material being taught at different points during the year, whether they had differentiated their instruction and had accommodated learning disabilities, and what personal issues in the lives of the students they believed might be having an effect on learning and subsequent assessment of that learning. Armed with a more complete picture of why the student recognition program wasn't as effective as expected, Nina would meet with the principal and discuss how to change their strategy.

The impetus to change professional practices comes from being convinced that there is a better way to help students learn successfully. Knowledge about how to find those answers through action research is power. When teachers feel caught between what they know how to do with confidence and what local, state, and federal mandates require them to do differently, they need specific strategies to restructure their practice and even to take proactive steps toward transforming school culture. Without a way to address the pressures they feel, teachers can become discouraged or, worse, despairing about the whole profession.

Changing one's practice happens as we are confronted with clear evidence that contradicts existing beliefs and assumptions. That perspectives and practices can change is demonstrated by Lizotte's (1998) action research study on the English as a Second Language Oral Assessment (ESOLA) being used in an adult education program in New Bedford, Massachusetts:

In conducting action research, I intended to demonstrate the limitations of the standardized testing (English as a Second Language Oral Assessment) used in our program. I approached the research with a preconceived opinion that a variety of more suitable tests would provide valid information about our students and be learner centered. . . . As I continued my research a whole new perspective emerged. The fault in the process was not the test itself; in fact the test was suited for its intended purpose. (p. 1)

This demonstrates the importance of being willing to challenge our own preconceived ideas as we progress and, through the process of action research, come to new understandings about assessment practices.

In another study on teacher research in Massachusetts, Larkin (2000) observed the process of change. Over a 3-year period, seven teachers and two college faculty members engaged in this collaborative project to investigate the relationship between theory and practice in an elementary school setting. Learning was a reciprocal process that also provided college faculty with real stories about teaching and learning as they taught and supervised preservice teachers. Larkin recorded her insights in a journal:

> It wasn't any particular feedback that occurred in the Inquiry Seminar itself that seemed to inspire changes to professional practice. Rather, it was the process of thinking about these topics combined with the structure of presenting, hearing encouragement, and sharing meanings with colleagues that served to push forward new ideas or possibilities. Having the forum to muck around with various interpretations of data and theoretical frameworks, and to trust that others would understand the difficulties and impediments to implementing anything earth shatteringly different, seemed to be essential to the outcome of changed teaching. As the Principal said one day when she had attended our Seminar meeting, "Change happens in the engagement with the question. 'What I'm thinking' may be the best evidence you get." (p. 350)

Larkin's study documented how the teachers' images of themselves shifted as they went from being consumers of research to producers of research in their own classrooms. One teacher wrote in her reflective journal:

> With the feedback and ideas from the group, I suddenly could perceive myself as a researcher as well as a teacher, and I realized how the researcher role can inform the teacher role in ways that I hadn't thought about, and this is very exciting. (p. 359)

In summary, Figure 7.2 outlines the sequence of steps and some possible activities that teachers can use in planning an action research project.

ADDITIONAL THOUGHTS

Stiggins (1997) points out that initial teacher preparation does not always include courses on assessment. Preparing new teachers to be action researchers would give them the tools to be reflective practitioners right from the start of their careers. They would be ready to collaboratively inquire

FIGURE 7.2. Planning an Action Research Project

Steps	*Possible Activities*		
Identify problems of practice	Brainstorm	Journal	Read
Focus the question	Form an action research group with colleagues	Discuss problems of practice collaboratively	Frame a problem in a specific question
Collect the data	Match strategies to question	Choose two or more methods	Decide on time line
Discuss interpretations	Cross-reference sources	Organize data to present	Interpret collectively
Take action and plan next steps	New teaching strategy?	New assessment strategy?	New inquiry question?

into their assessment practices in a structured, rigorous, and informed way so that they could respond proactively and positively to the reality of today's classrooms. Using action research as a means to "assess assessment" in the classroom can have exponential implications for teachers to continually "learn about learning" and can provide them with the wherewithal to answer their own questions and renew their professional practice throughout their teaching lives.

Within a community of learners, there is a safety net to take risks and opportunities for dialogue to clarify thinking. Being in the role of generating new knowledge, teachers experience personal growth and see themselves in a context of education that is broader than the reality of their own classrooms. The "teacher as researcher" is empowered by paying close attention to things that are puzzling, having a defined strategy for answering questions, and gaining insight into the dynamics of learning within the classroom (Larkin, 2000; McClean, 1997).

Collaboration to Strengthen Classroom Assessment

Janice Fauske

As I walked into Summerville Middle School, I paused a moment in the hallway outside the main office to take in the feel and flavor of the school; I often pause this way on my visits to administrative interns. Summerville was located in a low socioeconomic area of this medium-sized city and many of the students were children of factory workers and immigrants. The intern I was visiting exuded a passion and commitment for this school that inspired me to learn more about the children and teachers there. I saw a class passing quietly from the media center; their smiling teacher nodded as she passed. The immaculate hallway was filled with student artwork and brightly colored bulletin boards. Three women wearing labels reading "Parent Volunteers" were tutoring at several desks in an alcove. The secretary interrupted my perusal of the school by inviting me into the office. As I signed in, I heard voices discussing new test results and gains in reading that some children had made and how the 6th-grade team could work together to extend those gains to all 6th graders. The hallmarks of a positive school community were readily apparent, yet Summerville, for the second year, had been graded with an F by the state department of education on the basis of high stakes–testing scores. I was looking in vain for clues to explain why. Shouldn't F schools be noticeably different from the A and B schools I had visited earlier that day? Shouldn't an experienced educator be able to see the differences immediately?

As schools are increasingly placed under pubic scrutiny for ensuring adequate yearly progress of their students, the practice of rating schools by grades or numeric indicators similarly increases. A school's grade is an interpretation of aggregated scores of individual students on standardized tests. This practice overgeneralizes the findings and goes beyond what the data from any one measure can legitimately tell. Without essential understanding of individual student scores, revealing classroom assessments, and school community context, school rating can do little to either explain or affect teaching and learning. Instead, it often creates tension, frustration, and fear.

Thus, one of the inherent propositions of standardized, high-stakes testing is an omnipresent influence on school culture. Individual student scores are easily aggregated into assessment by grade levels and whole schools as well as by individual teachers. Schools can be publicly identified as failing, and teachers or grade levels can be targeted as weak. Such practices have fierce effects on the enthusiasm and vigor of educators. Only when the assessment results are effectively used to build up rather than tear down morale can the school expect to preserve the vitality of its staff. Positive, growth-inducing measures for getting the most out of assessment data can provide a robust impetus for crafting a professional culture of inquiry, shared practice, and community.

The authors of the first several chapters in the present volume discussed assessment ranging from individual student assessment to classroom, district, and state-mandated tests. In this chapter, I explore school-level interpretation of both these assessment results. The focus is on teachers' coalescing around systematic data collection and interpretation for continual improvement of instruction in relation to indicated student needs. Examples of ways to organize the school for best uses of assessment data and profiles as well as methods for directly informing instructional practice will be outlined. I then offer examples of teachers' organizing within schools in a collaborative response to assessment results that creates a school culture of reciprocal support among teachers and a seamless safety net for student learning. The discussion is guided by several questions:

1. How do effective schools interpret assessment data in ways that shape instruction and learning outcomes?
2. What are the characteristics of culture and community in schools where teachers collaborate for continual improvement of teaching and learning?
3. How do teachers learn the process of continual reflection and improvement on teaching?

OPPORTUNITY FOR DIALOGUE AND COMMUNITY BUILDING

Although often viewed as stress inducing, the continued emphasis of standardized testing in the assessment of students allows teachers and schools to create opportunities for dialogue about teaching and learning that, in turn, can engender an atmosphere of collegiality and cooperation in schools. The logic of accountability through assessment infers that publicizing student scores invites scrutiny from a variety of constituencies, including the teachers themselves. The assumption is that knowing how students are performing on this measure can inform the ongoing monitoring of student learning and the effectiveness of instructional choices. Yet experienced educators know that a single indicator cannot tell the whole story of student progress.

When we combine these high-stakes data with the plethora of contextual factors and conditions that shape the assessment results for students and schools, educators can begin to talk earnestly about the instructional process and about shared goals for student learning. This reflective dialogue is a cornerstone for building professional community in schools (DuFour & Eaker, 1998; Hord, 1997; Louis & Kruse, 1995) that can produce a collective response to student needs as identified through holistic and authentic assessment. In professional learning communities, educators become a community of learners who use data reflectively and in concert with other factors to make decisions about instruction. The school community can support or hinder the development of professional community.

When Ms. Shaw took her first principalship just a year ago at Summerville, she was determined to implement the strategies that her mentor principal had at Wilshire Elementary. The mentor principal had established several teams of teachers, counselors, paraprofessionals, and other staff, as well as parents. The teams had been charged with various responsibilities for ensuring student success at Wilshire, ranging from student learning to a safe and orderly environment. For example, teacher teams concentrated on improving instruction based on student achievement profiles created from a combination of standardized and classroom tests as well as teacher observations. Parents formulated volunteer schedules and coordinated business partnerships. The custodians and bus drivers participated in safety meetings. To Ms. Shaw, the constant buzz of meetings, activities, and changes felt somewhat chaotic, yet she sensed a positive atmosphere at the school that was pervasive and contagious. She wondered how a principal could keep up with it all. Ms. Shaw soon discovered the secret. The mentor principal had learned over time that, in the face of continual budget shortages, his most precious and primary resource was human, in the form of motivation, energy, commitment, and creativity. Put simply, the principal respected, nurtured, and trusted people in the school community, and he knew that student success depended on many people working together. He maintained a delicate balance of guiding and supporting his teams, and, by garnering the collective creativity and power of the teams, he moved the school forward. Ms. Shaw had seen similar progress during her first 2 years at Summerville. A strategy helpful to Ms. Shaw and her mentor principal is a process that focuses on the assessment and evaluation of such a professional learning community in their schools. This process highlights both strengths and areas of need, which in turn informs future developments of the professional learning community.

Certain factors are indicators of an authentic engagement of educators, of a community that consistently exchanges information about students and reflects on ways to improve student learning. Several studies have explored those factors and offer similar findings. Four complementary studies provide a framework for understanding professional learning communities and the ways that educators interact in those communities.

- Louis and Kruse (1995) describe professional learning communities in schools as exhibiting five characteristics: (1) collaboration, working together toward a common purpose; (2) reflective dialogue, learning from data and practice; (3) deprivatization of practice, opening one's teaching to scrutiny; (4) a constant, pervasive focus on student learning; and (5) shared values for what is important and how resources should be directed.
- Hord (1997), who has studied professional learning communities for more than 10 years, recognizes five indicators of professional learning communities: (1) supportive and shared leadership with leaders who are knowledgeable and committed to building community, (2) collective creativity and freedom to "think outside the box," (3) shared values accompanied by a shared vision for the school, (4) supportive conditions, and (5) shared teaching practice.
- DuFour and Eaker's (1998) findings, made more credible by Du-Four's firsthand experience as a high school principal and a superintendent, identify six characteristics: (1) shared mission, vision, and values; (2) collective inquiry; (3) numerous collaborative teams; (4) an orientation toward action research and experimentation; (5) continuous improvement; and (6) a continual search for results.
- Fauske (2002) studied three middle schools for more than 2 years, focusing in particular on the influence of school leaders on the

organization of the schools. She found that certain conditions were present in schools where collaboration and professional community flourished: (1) school leaders overtly supported and participated in collaboration, (2) teamwork became recognized in the evaluation and reward structures, (3) ongoing structures (advisory groups, committees, schedules, etc.) were established to facilitate collaborative work, (4) consensus on shared values and vision was intentionally built, and (5) the forums and patterns for collaborative work became customary and expected.

Each set of findings varies slightly, but all the findings have unifying themes that lend themselves to a checklist that can be used to guide both an assessment of the nature and extent of professional community in schools. These findings are synthesized in Figure 8.1 as a checklist of indicators that can help assess the level of professional community, particularly with regard to student learning and instructional improvement. Figure 8.1 offers school leaders, both formally assigned administrators and teacher leaders, a systematic way of assessing the various elements of professional community and identifying areas of focus for school improvement.

FIGURE 8.1. Tool 1: Professional Learning Communities in School

Characteristic/Condition Scale	*Commendations/Recommendations*
1. Shared values, vision and language that focus on student success Absent ___ Occasional___ Consistent___	
2. Culture of creativity, inquiry, and openness to new ideas Absent ___ Occasional___ Consistent___	
3. Genuine and authentic participation by school community Absent ___ Occasional___ Consistent___	
4. Multiple opportunities, structures and recognition for reflection and dialogue Absent ___ Occasional___ Consistent___	
5. Consistent in directing energy and resources toward achieving results Absent ___ Occasional___ Consistent___	

TEACHERS REFLECTING AND LEARNING TOGETHER

A major focus of professional learning communities is teachers' continual focus on student success. Teachers are the conduits for merging testing data with a variety of classroom-based assessment to produce a holistic profile of learning for each student. They can make good decisions for the student learning through careful consideration of these data by learning to be reflective about their instructional strategies and through dialogue focused on sharing ideas with other teachers. Because teachers are the primary vehicles through which assessment, instructional, and adaptation dialogue occurs, much of the discussion here focuses on the role of teachers in professional learning communities and how teachers learn habits of reflection, inquiry, creativity, and openness.

Reflection in teaching has been discussed as a goal for preparation of teachers for more than 2 decades. Schön's (1983, 1987) *The Reflective Practitioner* describes *reflection in action,* when teachers assess and adjust their practice during teaching—as with checks for understanding—and *reflection on action,* when teachers look back on their practice to assess its efficacy. Reflection in this definition involves critically examining a teaching process and the student response embedded in the context of the classroom and the school. To Schön, reflective practitioners think through a process, examining their own assumptions, beliefs, and understandings while allowing themselves to experience confusion and puzzlement (ambiguity). Then, practitioners experiment—either in reality or hypothetically (as in planning)—with changes in their practices based on the reflective assessment.

Critical reflection among both prospective and practicing teachers emerges through communities of peers engaged in dialogue about educational issues (Calderhead & Gates, 1993; Putnam & Borko, 2000; Wade & Fauske, 2004). Such dialogue allows for a safe space for experimenting with ideas or strategies, and it hones our ability to reason, "especially our ability to solve problems, to think sensibly toward conclusions, to weigh competing considerations, and to choose reasonable courses of action" (Dewey, 1914/1944, p. 11). Dialogue is valuable because it helps us to see and consider a situation "as another would see it, considering what points of contact it has with the life of another" (Dewey, 1914/1944, p. 6). Dialogue is highly valued in the professional development of teachers who introduce a richness of experience, strategies, and means of assessment into a "community" of discourse, each teacher learning from other teachers and creating a richer understanding of teaching and learning (Putnam & Borko, 2000). Dewey emphasized that teachers who reflect collaboratively develop a shared sense of priorities, consider alternative views or solutions, and offer mutual support for ongoing reflection and continual improvement (Rodgers, 2003). They create an individual habit of being continually aware of their choices and actions as well as the impacts on students. When this habit becomes shared across teachers and other teams of educators, including staff and parents, the culture of the school begins to exhibit characteristics of a professional community.

COLLECTIVE INTERPRETATION OF DATA
FOR INSTRUCTIONAL IMPROVEMENT

Deprivatizing practice, or sharing individual teaching strategies and results, emerges from reflection and dialogue among educators. Teachers begin to examine their assessment and teaching practices and make adjustments in instruction. When this process is directly tied to assessment data, it has the potential to powerfully affect the instructional-improvement process by providing an opportunity to set shared educational goals (Rosenholtz, 1991; Schmoker, 2001, 2003). Setting shared goals is another important element of a professional learning community. As teachers examine their classroom-based assessment data in comparison with the standardized-testing data, which lacks specificity and has a blurred relationship with instruction, they identify school- or grade-level strengths and areas of need. From these strengths and areas of need, teachers can determine where to focus their energies for the greatest impact on student learning. The resulting changes in teaching go well beyond reteaching concepts or skills to developing corrective instruction designed to remedy both content and learning deficiencies identified through their analysis (Guskey, 2003). They may discover, for example, that 5th-grade students excel in vocabulary and spelling but lag behind in writing proficiency. Those teachers may then set a collective goal for improvement of writing skills across the 4th grade. Implementation of strategies to reach the goal falls to each teacher, who is supported by continued dialogue with other teachers, sharing of ideas and strategies, planned professional development activities related to the shared goal, and systematic assessments across the classrooms.

The impact of dialogue around assessment, then, reaches instruction in three ways:

1. Individual teachers reflect on their own practices, collect classroom-based assessment data, review standardized assessments, discuss these data with other teachers, and make fundamental adjustments to instruction, not simply reteaching, but rethinking their teaching practice.
2. Teachers examine standardized data for groups of students, compare it with their classroom-based data, identify strengths and deficiencies, and set shared instructional goals for groups of students (cluster, grade, and school level).
3. These activities, in turn, create a schoolwide culture of reflective dialogue, a professional learning community that provides a safe and productive space for a continual cycle of improvement.

Teachers trust the results of classroom-based assessments, the quizzes, tests, writing assignments, and related learning activities that they use regularly in the classroom (Guskey, 2003). They value the importance of context, of knowing their students' backgrounds and abilities. Only when the strengths of teachers are merged with the standardized data that rank and order students and schools can we hope to set and attain meaningful instructional goals and learning gains across groups of students at grade levels and ultimately at the school level.

Ms. Shaw has created several opportunities for teachers to be trained in effective observation and feedback techniques. Teachers at Summerville regularly visit one another's classrooms; offer feedback; and share ideas through nondirective communication, brainstorming, and group dialogue. Ms. Shaw sets aside time at faculty meetings for teacher exchange, including asking for feedback and assistance with problems as well as prioritizing needs for future professional development. Ms. Shaw participates in these professional development activities alongside her teachers. She has also learned parallel-observation and feedback techniques for school leaders. She takes pride in the strides that her staff has made in creating a culture of openness and inquiry.

MAKING IT HAPPEN

Studies of teachers spending time in discussions and planning activities have revealed several impediments to developing professional learning communities (Conley, Fauske, & Pounder, 2004; Fauske & Schelble, 2002). These barriers fall into two major categories: (1) lack of time for dialogue, training, or developing expertise; and (2) unclear, inconsistent, or competing school or district priorities. Several measures, discussed in the following three sections, can be implemented to circumvent the negative effects of these barriers.

Time for Teacher Learning and Training

Teachers have little time for dialogue during the day. Their schedules are rigidly fixed around the bells and the movement of students from class to class, with scarcely an opportunity to exchange information about students or instruction. Teachers often squeeze such dialogue into rushed conversations between classes, before or after school, or over lunch. Time can be provided for exchanging important information about instruction and students in several creative ways.

In some places in the country, school districts have made districtwide schedule changes that provide time for collaboration among school personnel. In Utah, Salt Lake City District dismisses elementary students early on Wednesdays and middle school students early on Fridays for meetings of teacher teams, parent-teacher groups, and other groups that participate in decision making about students. Initially, some parents objected to the early dismissal, citing increased child-care problems. The district public relations staff rallied the community in support of the measure as necessary for the continual improvement of instruction and more effective, individualized monitoring of student progress. Some schools organized after-school programs, run by parent and community volunteers, to relieve some of the child-care issues.

Other districts, such as that of the University of California, Los Angeles elementary school, have built in up to 20 additional paid workdays for teachers and staff to support teaching and learning activities in schools (Raywid, 1993). Yet many districts have not taken such steps, and schools have to find time in creative ways. Figure 8.2 offers some creative options adapted and expanded from "Finding Time for Collaboration" (Raywid, 1993). These options can be the springboard for similar ideas that fit the context of particular schools and districts. In states where union contracts tightly govern the schedules of teachers, making changes within the school day is the primary option available. Even with limited flexibility in teachers' schedules, schools where teachers are committed to enriching dialogue about teaching and learning seem to find ways with work within the rules. The more formidable obstacle seems to be gaining commitment from the teachers themselves to the elements of professional community (Evans-Stout, 1998).

FIGURE 8.2. Tool 2: Making Time for Collaborative Responses

Schedule teachers with the same lunch time and/or planning.	Offer teachers compensatory time for meeting outside the school schedule.
Organize parents and paraprofessionals to supervise service or community learning.	Add paid instructional planning days for each grading period.
In large schools, increasing class size by 1–2 students can provide additional planning time for team leaders.	Switch excess instructional days (over the minimum required) to planning days.
Organize students in a single grade into two separate groups with separate teachers and combine groups for some activities with one set of teachers supervising.	Extend the school days on 4 days and dismiss students early one day per week.
Assign music, physical education, speech, computer, theater, and other classes to "supplemental" staff to create meeting time for core teachers. Supplemental teachers also have time to meet.	Extend class periods for a few minutes and dismiss students early one day per week; organize community activities for the early-out day.

Note: From Raywid (1993). Adapted with permission of the author.

When given time for dialogue, teachers can work toward collaborative decision-making with support and training in the process. Professional development on these collaborative processes must support learning at two levels: the conceptual and the procedural. The conceptual level involves the cognitive understanding of the nature and purposes of shared dialogue and the importance of professional community. The procedural level involves developing the behaviors, skills, and strategies required for effective collaboration. This level of learning must evolve over time as teachers make meaning of their own experience with participating in a professional community.

These two kinds of learning can occur together or independently of each other. Procedures are more readily changed than are their supporting conceptual assumptions and belief, but conceptual changes ensure more permanent, "deep," and long-lasting changes in teacher thinking. Teachers who have operated somewhat autonomously for many years may resist when beginning to participate in collaborative decision-making at the grade or school level. Instead of making decisions that affect only their students or a group of students that is shared by just a few other teachers (i.e., as in team teaching or in department-type decisions), they share in grade-level school-based decisions and activities. Such a shift in thinking has powerful implications for their work as teachers. The old measures of accountability and effectiveness, which tended to focus on such measures as observing teachers for evaluation, absence of serious discipline problems, evidence of planning, cleanliness of the room, and willingness to serve on a committee or two at the school level, now include performance of students on a variety of assessment indicators, willingness to share and receive information on instructional improvement, as well as effective communication skills (Sergiovanni, 1994). This shift to collaborative decision-making and collective responses to assessment and instructional needs nurtures the spirit of continual improvement.

Keeping the Focus Clear

Messages from the principal and from the district office must continually support and clarify the priority of collaboration for improving student performance. Most districts offer limited funds and opportunities for teachers' professional development. When professional growth and training activities for developing professional community are consistently highlighted as a priority, the breadth of learning about collaborative processes can take hold across many teachers and schools (Fauske, 1999; Fauske & Schelble, 2000). In this way, the school, and ultimately the whole district, can experience a level of shared learning and language about collaborative, team-based responses to students' learning needs. Thus, principals who initiate and support a community of inquiry, because of their individual beliefs and training, can facilitate the development of collaborative skills among teachers in that school. When several principals in a given district focus on the development of such a community, the culture of the district begins to embrace the notion of shared responsibility for student learning.

Creating the view of shared responsibility for student learning extends beyond the walls of the school into the community. When time is allotted for teacher dialogue and shared decision-making during regular school time, it is sometimes viewed as "nonteaching" time by parents and others who may lack understanding of the importance of dialogue and building professional community in schools. For some constituencies, only the time that teachers spend in front of students is considered teaching time. Overcoming this notion, even among teachers, requires creating new habits, new language, and new public relations strategies.

Respecting the Process

Strictly respecting the time, space, and integrity needed for the collaborative responses to student assessment and instructional needs can send a consistent message of the value and importance of maintaining professional community. Principals sometimes advocate for professional community and teacher dialogue about assessment, teaching, and learning while simultaneously allowing time for that dialogue to be usurped by extraneous matters and interruptions. Something as simple as a principal or fellow teacher dropping in on a team meeting to make a brief announcement can disrupt the flow of dialogue and send the message that such dialogue is a lesser priority (Fauske & Schelble, 2002). Principals can also undermine the process when ignoring or reversing teacher-made decisions (Fauske & Schelble, 2002).

Perhaps most important to setting and maintaining an emphasis on participation in collaborative decision-making about student assessment and learning is restructuring the teacher–evaluation process that traditionally focuses on individual teachers and classrooms rather than on out-of-classroom planning and dialogue. Including participation in collaborative decision-making for instructional improvement as a recognized and rewarded work of teachers can ensure the longevity of a genuine professional community.

Clearly, increasing emphasis on developing professional learning communities and growth in the number of schools implementing these processes are evidence of the need to change in our approach to assessment. Schools that are rich with dialogue and opportunities for exchange regarding student learning have recognized this need for more dialogue around student assessment and learning. A variety of models have emerged for structuring and facilitating such dialogue. One intriguing development is the implementation of class, grade, and school collaborative responses to generated data that is managed by a school data coach.

THE ROLE OF DATA COACHES

The imperative need for dialogue around student assessment and learning has precipitated a variety of approaches and models. Some schools and districts have chosen to use data coaches and have one or two teachers in each school trained to interpret and synthesize a variety of indicators of student learning and to translate those data for other teachers as a profile of student learning. That profile, in turn, can be linked to specific instructional responses as suggestions to the teachers. In some districts this process is supported with preprogrammed data displays and charts with built-in links to teaching ideas and resources. Teachers come together with the data coach to decide what indicators should be included in the student profile of learning; those indicators can then be compiled into a simple spreadsheet-style data display that shows the profile at a glance. Such data as standardized-test scores, classroom-based assessments, and other factors are displayed in a format that allows teachers to see the patterns for each student. These data displays are programmed to aggregate such data by classroom, grade level, school, and Adequate Yearly Progress (AYP) groups. Teachers can see patterns for a whole class, a group of students (such as students in 7th-grade math who have labels of special education), or an entire grade level. Teachers can discover that 4th-grade math students are weak in division of fractions, for example, and can make adjustments collectively in that area of instruction. Links to possible resources for teaching division of fractions are provided. The dialogue around this problem begins and the response follows. Teachers can also assess their own instructional patterns. If the grade-level data show patterns across a grade, a teacher who sees that her students do not compare well in a particular subject or skill can make adjustments; seek out resources; and, in a school with professional community, seek help from other teachers. Data coaching is one model for teachers responding to data collaboratively for student learning

PRINCIPLES FOR WHOLE-SCHOOL COLLABORATIVE RESPONSES TO ASSESSMENT

This chapter has emphasized the importance of dialogue and shared practice among teachers in a professional learning community with particular focus on sharing assessment data across teachers. I have acknowledged the place of standardized, classroom-based, and related assessments while honoring the pivotal role of teachers in successful student learning. Teachers reflecting through dialogue can influence assessment and instructional practices in three ways:

1. Reflecting on their own practices, discussing assessment and instruction with other teachers, and making adjustments to their own instruction;

2. Examining, with other teachers, assessment data for individuals and groups of students to identify strengths and deficiencies and to set shared instructional goals for groups of students; and
3. Creating a schoolwide culture of reflective dialogue—a professional learning community.

Together, these form guiding principles for nurturing collaborative responses to assessment data generated in schools. Teachers merge classroom data that they inherently trust with standardized data to refine instructional practice and assessment in a cycle of continual improvement. Such authentic and meaningful collaboration develops a powerful process for monitoring and enhancing student learning.

# Involving Parents in Classroom Assessment

Phyllis Jones

Two moms, Rose and Sylvia, have walked out of school after morning drop-off; Rose approaches Sylvia in the parking lot. This is the conversation that ensues.

Rose: Are you going to the parent information meeting tonight?

Sylvia: No, not tonight—we have soccer and [the meeting is] about assessment, which has all been decided anyway. . . . When have they ever taken notice of us? We're just the parents, you know.

Rose: I know what you mean. . . . I had Derek's annual review of his IEP [Individualized Education Plan] last week and do you know what happened? . . . They had everything decided before I entered the room. Everything was typed up and all they wanted from me was my signature. I was so upset that I couldn't say anything and since then I have become more and more angry about it.

Sylvia: Oh, how awful! . . . Did you agree with everything they had decided?

Rose: Well, everything sort of stayed the same as last year, but I really wanted to talk about Derek's assessment and progress in literacy. He has been going to Boy Scouts and his scoutmaster says that he is having difficulty with the signs in the manual. I had hoped to discuss that with the teachers and perhaps form a goal around it . . . but there was no room on the form and no time to discuss anything that wasn't on the form—it really was frustrating.

Sylvia: I'm sorry. . . . Sometimes I think those teachers forget that we are the parents and that we know our children . . . and that our children have a life outside of school. It all seems to be about this score here and that score there. . . . Surely our children are more than a score!

Rose: Yeah, you're right. . . . I'm not going to the parent information meeting, either . . . waste of my time. Enjoy soccer practice!

Sylvia: Will do. . . . At least the coach listens to me. Seriously, though, you really should say something about that meeting you went to. It should not happen like that.

Rose: I know. You're right again. . . . But when will they ever listen to parents? Perhaps when pigs fly!

Both moms walk to their respective cars laughing.

This vignette tells of a worst-case scenario where two parents have had experiences with schools that have made them reluctant to become more involved and learn more about assessment. The parent information meeting may have offered the parents valuable insight into different assessment processes in the school, but previous experiences are guiding the parents' perspectives and actions. In this chapter, I analyze some of the reasons why teachers should want to involve parents in classroom assessments, and then I provide practical ways in which teachers can do this; further, I explore potential questions a parent may have regarding the assessment policies and practices in school, along with possible responses a teacher may give to such questions.

RATIONALE

Parents have an active role to play in the assessment of their children in school. Historically, this role has been mainly viewed as an "after the fact" reporting of progress and achievement by the teacher to the parent. For students with disabilities, parents have often been seen as integral participants in the stages of referral to formative eligibility for additional services and in the process of developing an IEP (Hundt, 2002). As teachers develop a broader and more holistic view of assessment in the classroom, the importance of parental involvement in the process of ongoing assessment for all children is becoming more accepted (McConnell & Odum, 1999; Villa & Thousand, 2005). In an assessment model that moves from a convergent perspective, focused on the summative purposes of assessment, to a more divergent perspective, focused on the different ways children's learning can be acknowledged and celebrated, the ongoing involvement of parents in real and meaningful ways is crucial. This involves the building and sharing of authentic and alternative assessments of students (Carr, 2004). It is not enough for parents simply to be present; teachers need to facilitate active participation in the assessment process in order to (Wolfendale, 2004):

- Enable parents and teachers to participate in target-setting together in order that the opportunities for transferal of learning between school and home increase;
- Enable parents to be more aware of curricular content and goals;
- Enable parents to become more knowledgeable about how their child is responding at school and to be in a better position to support teacher endeavors;

- Help teachers to become more aware of how a student is responding at home; and
- Help students to appreciate that parents and teachers are communicating and working together for their well-being.

In short, parental involvement in classroom assessment is both worthwhile and valuable for the teacher, the parent, and ultimately the student. Indeed, in a recent research project (Trepanier-Street, 2001), teachers of students in early years and elementary schools, when asked about involving parents in classroom assessment, stated that such a level of involvement was not only essential, but must be a summative and ongoing process, something affirmed in the work of Carnie (2004).

FACILITATING GREATER PARENT INVOLVEMENT IN CLASSROOM ASSESSMENT

In order to facilitate greater participation by parents in classroom assessment, we need to consider what is occurring now and how this could be increased in the future. Currently there is a major emphasis on the reporting of classroom assessments from teachers to parents. This includes formative assessment, summative assessment, attainment testing, standardized testing, and national testing, with reporting occurring through school reports, grade sheets, home–school letters, multimedia usage (such as teacher websites), and face-to-face meetings. To increase greater involvement, teachers need to invite parental participation in the assessment process at an earlier stage and in an appropriate way. For example, it is highly appropriate for parents to contribute actively to content-specific preassessment that has the potential to inform the teachers' planning and teaching. Figure 9.1 offers an example of a form that invites parents to share information on previous experience students may have in relation to the work they are going to be doing.

It is crucial to dispel the illusion that assessment is the sole responsibility of the classroom teacher by increasing parental understanding of assessment in the classroom. One way to do this is to involve parents in key assessment processes. Clearly this has to be paced and managed so that the process is feasible and not overwhelming for teachers and parents. Figure 9.2 offers a suggestion of a form that could be adopted for this. In this form, the parent is not only informed about the curriculum goals and the student levels of engagement, but also is invited to add comments.

FIGURE 9.1. Form for Parental Involvement in Preassessment

Student name:

Topic:

Key questions and curriculum standards addressed in topic:

•

•

Examples of student experience as it relates to key questions of the topic:

•

•

Additional parent comments:

Signed and dated:

Parent: _____

Teacher: _____

FIGURE 9.2. Form for Parental Involvement in Assessment of Topic Achievement

Student name:

Topic:

Key questions and curriculum standards addressed in topic:

•

•

Examples of how student's work relates to key questions:

•

•

Parent comment:

Teacher comment:

Signed and dated:

Parent: _____

Teacher: _____

When inviting parents to be part of the assessment process, it is important to be clear and reassuring to parents from the outset. Bearing this in mind, it may be helpful to consider potential questions parents may have about the assessment experience of their child and, in considering possible responses to such questions, ensure that a message of parental value is conveyed in the answer.

INVOLVING PARENTS OF STUDENTS WITH LEARNING DIFFERENCES

In the diverse classrooms of today, it is usual to have students in the class who have identified or nonidentified learning differences. These may involve students whose first language is not English, students with identified disabilities, students identified as gifted, and students who are not identified but who have clear learning differences and require an Academic Improvement Plan (AIP). Rose, a mother in the vignette at the beginning of the chapter, really wanted to participate actively in her son's evaluation but felt powerless to do so. With students who learn differently a teacher may be responsible, in collaboration with other teachers, staff, and professionals, for managing the formal and informal assessment processes. This may take many forms but could potentially include being involved in a child study team, an IEP team, a behavior support team, an English for speakers of other languages (ESOL) planning and intervention team, or more informal meetings throughout the year to assess ongoing progress.

Teachers may also be involved in alternative and alternate assessment processes linked to the No Child Left Behind Act of 2001 (NCLB). Indeed, this legislation "requires schools to develop ways to get parents more involved in their child's education and in improving the school" (NCLB, 2001). This is rapidly becoming a natural part of each and every teacher's general responsibilities as the diversity in classrooms increases. It is crucial that parents' views and involvement are nurtured in a process that many parents may find overwhelming and intimidating. In order to do this, it may be important to ensure that parents have the appropriate support required to participate in the meeting. For some parents this may involve an interpreter being present and with others it may involve more sustained support before, during, and after the assessment meeting. Jones and Swain (2001) worked with a group of parents of children with identified learning differences and highlighted guidelines for teachers who wished to involve parents effectively in such assessment processes:

- Be jargon free as much as possible.
- Be willing to spend time building relationships with parents.
- Do not be oversensitive and reactive to perspectives of parents.
- Share expertise with parents; try to develop a working alliance and make joint decisions.
- Know the whole child; parents know when teachers do not really know their children.
- Help parents to prepare for meetings.
- Manage meetings so that they are less formal, and do not have decisions made beforehand.

Returning to Rose's incident in the vignette, if these guidelines had been followed, she would have had a very different experience at the annual review of her son, Derek. Dabowski (2004) suggests that to improve parental involvement and participation in a child's annual review system, it is essential to reflect and evaluate on team practices and cultures in the school. In reviewing these guidelines and the need to reflect continually upon the culture of participation that schools foster, it is clear that such fundamental principles apply to all students in all classrooms.

SUPPORTING PARENTS
IN ASKING QUESTIONS ABOUT ASSESSMENT

When parents enter schools, they may come with lots of questions that they want to explore in their meeting with teachers. It may be beneficial to prepare a fact sheet to distribute to parents (in home languages) before the meeting, as this may help to support parents to know what information they need to discuss at the meeting. It would also be helpful to be prepared for questions. A fact sheet could be developed from the range of questions and possible responses outlined below. Teachers could develop the fact sheet in relation to the focus of the upcoming assessment meeting. A variety of fact sheets can be developed using some of the questions and responses below, depending upon the focus of the meeting:

- For a general introduction to the role of parents in assessment, sample questions 1, 2, and 3 may be useful.
- For a meeting focusing on assessment in the classroom for groups of diverse learners, sample questions 1, 2, and 5 may be applicable.

- For a meeting focusing upon specific upcoming assessments, sample questions 1, 2, 3, and 4 may be valuable.

Sample Question 1: Why would I want to be involved in my child's assessment?

Parents know their children better than anyone. The depth of knowledge they possess and the quality of relationship they enjoy makes parents an ideal partner in assessment and teaching in the classroom. Specifically, when parents become more involved in assessment, they will be able to

- Share learning goals with their child;
- Participate in the continual review and reflection of progress; and
- Provide quality feedback about their child in school, both formally and informally.

Sample Question 2: How can I become involved in assessment?

It may be helpful for parents to begin a home portfolio of the assessments their child brings home from school; through this they will naturally notice patterns emerging over time. If parents have questions or observations they would like to share, they should send a note to the teacher at any time. They may be invited, at times, to contribute to student preassessment and progress with particular curriculum topics, which may be done through surveys that will be sent home for completion and return. If there is particular concern about a child's progress and a parent wishes to initiate a formal assessment for additional provision of services, perhaps relating to an AIP or IEP, he or she will be invited to participate in this assessment process. In relation to a curriculum topic, the perspectives parents provide about their child will help the teacher to plan appropriate and challenging teaching and learning situations for the child.

Sample Question 3: What are the implications of assessment for my child and me?

Teachers use assessment in the classroom to help plan teaching and to monitor and celebrate individual progress through the curriculum. Assessment results help to give information about a child in relation to the curriculum and in relation to other children of a similar age. The implications of assessment results are therefore individual, as they relate to the child's individual progress. For example, results may reveal that a child is excelling in a particular area and would benefit from enhanced curricular experiences. Or they may indicate that a child, for some reason, is struggling in a particular area and requires parents and teachers to work together to understand why and put additional support into place. There is also mandatory standardized testing. This information is required by the district and state. It is an important indication of how a child is doing in relation to other students in his or her grade level. This information is also used by the district and state to see how well a school is performing and if it is meeting Adequate Yearly Progress (AYP).

Sample Question 4: How do I best prepare my child for assessment?

The most important thing to do is to convey calm to the child and respond positively to classroom and school assessments as everyday occurrences in teaching and learning. Assessment is not intended to be stressful, but some students do become anxious. Most assessment occurs in the natural environment of the classroom routine. It is helpful for a child to be well rested, well fed, and hydrated. Some teachers may send requests home for mints or chewing gum, which some teachers believe to be helpful in supporting focus and extended concentration.

Sample Question 5: My child has an IEP and has to have accommodations to his assessment—what does that mean for him or her in class?

Accommodations are changes to the administration of an assessment. They can include changes in time allowance, print size, and other presentation issues and also how a child needs to respond. For example, schools may offer an enlarged format of a test, which is split into discrete visual sections so that the test itself is not overwhelming visually. It is the IEP team, of which parents are crucial participants, that decides what the accommodations need to be, and these are specified on the IEP. A child will not notice anything different, as these accommodations link to the instructional accommodations used every day in the classroom. Parents may also hear about modifications. These often get confused with accommodations but are very different. A *modification* is a substantial change to *what* is being assessed and something different is given as an assessment of progress. For example, a modification may occur when a student is given a spell checker for a spelling test or a calculator on a computation test in math. Again, it is the IEP team that decides on such modifications, and again, these modifications will reflect what is already happening in the classroom.

CONCLUDING THOUGHTS

It is in the consideration of the issues raised in this chapter relating to why and how parents can be more involved in assessment, how to share assessment results with parents, and the potential parental questions and teacher responses to such questions that we begin to explore the complex nature of parental involvement in this important aspect of a child's school life. It is through such consideration, by inviting and using parental participation in assessment, that teachers will prevent the development of the situation described in the vignette. In doing so, teachers can demonstrate that, through working alliances between teachers and parents in assessment practices, the opportunities for transferal of learning between school and home increase. Such increases include

- Building up parental awareness of curricular content and goals;
- Enabling parents to become more knowledgeable about how their child is responding at school and thus support teacher endeavors;
- Helping teachers to become more aware of how a student is responding at home; and
- Helping students to appreciate that parents and teachers are communicating and working together for their well-being.

Through this, teachers and schools demonstrate a commitment to involve others in assessment practices, and in so doing create a more comprehensive process.

Afterword

Stephen Graves

We began in the introduction by stating that this book is primarily intended for practicing teachers, administrators, and preservice teachers. We believe that we have succeeded in providing a wealth of information about the processes, types, characteristics, and uses of classroom assessment. We hope that we have given the readers tools and examples that illustrate the benefits of using a variety of assessment strategies. The authors have used a research base to describe the values of using appropriate, meaningful assessments. Recognition of the importance of using assessments to make informed decisions about teaching and learning has been highlighted throughout the book.

Another salient point of the book is that terminology related to assessment needs clarification. As mentioned in Chapter 6, because such terms as *measurement, assessment, evaluation,* and *testing* have different meanings, they should not be used interchangeably. The book will help teachers understand the wide variety of assessment tools that exist and the multidimensional characteristics that differentiate the purposes and uses of these tools.

Another theme is to remind readers that because learning is diverse among students, we want to maximize each learner's strengths by choosing the best type of assessment. In recognizing the influence of children's language, culture, and experiences on their learning, teachers will consider the potential for bias in the assessment's approach. Accommodations and modifications in the assessment process may also be needed to ensure that teaching and learning are successful. An additional thread in the discussion points to how classroom assessment can and should be used to determine what students know and understand, as well as how they learn. A wide variety of approaches are presented here to serve as a basis for rethinking assumptions about assessment in general.

An examination of the key questions of what to assess, how to assess, and why we should assess learning is included. For example, selected assessments allow teachers to create profiles of children as learners. On another level, teachers may work collaboratively using dialogue and re-flection to gain insight into their own classroom assessment practices. Collegial discussions of best practices, professional development activities, sharing values for what resources are needed, and how they should be directed and focusing on student learning can help build learning com-munities. As teachers in such learning communities begin to critically examine their teaching and assessment practices in relation to positively influencing instruction, the potential is great to improve student learn-ing. This, of course, is of utmost importance. Teachers also use inquiry questions and action research to improve teaching and learning processes. Engaging parents in partnerships can produce positive results as well.

Whether we discuss the assessment of an individual child, a class-room, a school, a school district, a state system, or beyond, the topic of assessment will continue to be important to educators and the general public. We do not think the focus on assessment or accountability will be diminished over the coming decades. Our hope is that we, as educators, will keep the issues surrounding assessment in a balanced perspective and that the focus for using appropriate strategies will remain on improving instruction and learning. Finally, as we strive to balance assessment in classroom practice, we must believe that "a pig don't get fatter the more you weigh it." Assessing more often won't necessarily help us, but using the right tools will.

References

Abrams, J., Ferguson, J., & Laud, L. (2001). Assessing ESOL students. *Educational Leadership, 59*(3), 62–65.

Adams, M. J. (1994/1996). *Beginning to read: Thinking and learning about print.* Cambridge: Massachusetts Institute of Technology Press.

Adams, T. (1998). Alternative assessment in elementary school mathematics. *Childhood Education, 74*(4), 220–224.

Airasian, P.W. (2000) *Assessment in the classroom: A concise approach.* Boston: McGraw-Hill.

Alaska Department of Education. (1996). *Assessment in mathematics: Self and peer evaluations.* Retrieved October 6, 2005, from www.educ.state.ak.us/tls/frameworks/mathsci/ms5_2as2.htm

American Educational Research Association. (2000). Position statement of the American Educational Research Association concerning high-stakes testing in PreK–12 education. *Educational Researcher, 29*(8), 24–25.

American Educational Research Association, American Psychological Association, & National Council on Measurement in Education. (1999). *Standards for educational and psychological testing.* Washington, DC: American Psychological Association.

Applebee, A (1979). *The child's concept of story: Ages 2 to 17.* Chicago: University of Chicago Press.

Ascher, C. (1990). *Assessing bilingual students for placement and instruction.* New York: ERIC Clearing House on Urban Education. (ERIC Document Reproduction Service No. ED 322274). Retrieved December 8, 2005, from http://iume.tc.columbia.edu/eric_archive/digest/65.pdf

Banks, S. R. (2005). *Classroom assessment: Issues and practices.* Boston: Allyn & Bacon.

Bear, D. R., Invernizzi, M., Templeton, S., & Johnston, F. (2004). *Words their way: Word study for phonics, vocabulary, and spelling* (3rd ed.). Upper Saddle River, NJ: Prentice Hall.

Berg, B. L. (2001). *Qualitative research methods for the social sciences.* Needham Heights, MA: Allyn & Bacon.

Bialystok, E., Shenfield, T., & Codd, J. (2000). Languages, scripts, and the environment: Factors in developing concepts of print. *Developmental Psychology, 36*(1), 66–76.

Bishop, A., & Jones, P. (2002). Promoting inclusive practice in primary initial teacher training: Influencing hearts as well as minds. *Support for Learning, 17*(2), 58–64.

Black, P., Harrison, C., Lee, C., Marshall, B., & Wiliam, D. (2003). *Assessment for learning: Putting it into practice.* Buckingham, UK: Open University Press.

Blair, T. R. (2003). *New teacher's performance-based guide to culturally diverse classrooms.* Boston: Allyn & Bacon.

Bogdan, R. C., & Biklen, S. K. (2003). *Qualitative research for education* (4th ed.). Boston: Allyn & Bacon.

Brookhart, S. M. (1997). A theoretical framework for the role of classroom assessment in motivating student effort and achievement. *Applied Measurement In Education, 10*(2), 161–180.

Brookhart, S., Adnolina, M., Zuza, M., & Furman, R. (October 2004). Minute math: An action research study of student self-assessment. *Educational Studies in Mathematics, 57*(2), 213–227.

Browder, D., Flowers, C., Ahlgrim-Delzell, L., Karvonen, M., Spooner, F., & Algozzine, R. (2004). The alignment of alternative assessment content with academic and functional curricula. *Journal of Special Education, 37*(4), 211–223.

Bullough, R. V., & Gitlin, A. (1995). *Becoming a student of teaching.* New York: Garland.

Caine, R. N., & Caine, G. (1997). *Unleashing the power of perceptual change: The potential of brain-based teaching.* Alexandria, VA: Association for Supervision and Curriculum Development.

Calderhead, J., & Gates, P. (Eds.). (1993). *Conceptualizing reflection in teacher development.* London: The Falmer Press.

Cambell, B., Campbell, L., & Dickinson, D. (1999). *Teaching and learning through multiple intelligences.* Upper Saddle River, NJ: Prentice Hall.

Carey, L. (2001). *Measuring and evaluating school learning* (3rd ed.). Boston: Allyn & Bacon.

Carnie, F. (2004). *Pathways to child-friendly schools: A guide for parents.* Bristol, UK: Human Scale Education.

Carr, J. F., & Harris, D. E. (2001). *Succeeding with standards: Linking curriculum, assessment, and action planning.* Alexandria, VA: Association for Supervision and Curriculum Development.

Carr, M. (2004). A folk model of assessment and an alternative. In L. Miller & J. Devereux (Eds.), *Supporting children's learning in the early years* (pp. 54–66). London: David Fulton.

Cartledge, G., & Loe, S. A. (2001). Cultural diversity and social skill instruction. *Exceptionality, 9*(1/2), 33–46.

Castagnera, E., Fisher, D., Rodifer, K., & Sax, C. (1998). *Deciding what to teach and how to teach it: Connecting students through curriculum and instruction.* Colorado Springs, CO: PEAK Parent Center.

Chiappe, P., Siegel, L. S., & Gottardo, A. (2002). Reading-related skills of kindergartners from diverse linguistic backgrounds. *Applied Psycholinguistics, 23*(1), 95–116.

Clay, M. (2002). *An observation survey of early literacy achievement.* Portsmouth, NH: Heinemann.

Cohen, N. E., & Pompa, D. (1996). Multicultural perspectives on quality in early care and education: Culturally specific practices and universal outcomes. (Working paper). New Haven, CT: Yale University Press.

Conley, S., Fauske, J. R., & Pounder, D. (2004). Organizational context, work design, and interpersonal processes: Testing predictors of work group effectiveness. *Educational Administration Quarterly, 41*(2), 144–169.

Corey, S. M. (1953). *Action research to improve school practices.* New York: Teachers College Press.

Cunningham, P., & Allington, R. (2003). *Classrooms that work: They can all read and write* (3rd ed.). Boston: Pearson.

Dabowski, D.M. (2004). Encouraging active parent participation in IEP meetings. *Teaching Exceptional Children, 36*(3), 34–39.

Derwing, T., & Munro, M. J. (2001). What speaking rates do non-native listeners prefer? *Applied Linguistics, 22*(3), 324–337.

Dewey, J. (1944). *How we think.* Amherst, NY: Prometheus Books. (Original work published 1914)

Diamond, M., & Hopson, J. (1998). *Magic trees of the mind: How to nurture your child's intelligence, creativity, and healthy emotions from birth through adolescence.* New York: Penguin Putman.

Dodge, D. T., Heroman, C., & Charles, J. (2004). Beyond outcomes: How ongoing assessment supports children's learning and leads to meaningful curriculum. *Young Children, 59*(1), 20–28.

Downing, J., & Oliver, P. (1973). The child's conception of word. *Reading Research Quarterly, 9,* 568–582.

DuFour, R., & Eaker, R. (1998). *Professional learning communities at work: Best practices for enhancing student achievement.* Bloomington, IN: National Educational Service.

Einstein, A. (1929). *The history of field theory (olds and news of field theory).* Retrieved October 11, 2004, from http://www.rain.org/~karpeles/einsteindis.html

Eitelgeorge, J. S. (1994). *Writing development: A longitudinal study of multiple continua of conceptual understanding within the writing process as displayed by 1st grade writers.* Unpublished manuscript, Ohio State University, Columbus, OH.

Eitelgeorge, J. S. (2002). *Ongoing, informal literacy assessments: Assessments and instructional methods for monitoring and enhancing progress in literacy development.* Boston: Pearson.

Eitelgeorge, J. S., & Barrett, R. (2004). Multiple continua of development in a first grade classroom. *Reading Research and Instruction, 43*(2), 17–64.

Eitelgeorge, J. S., & Kent, K. (2001). *The ongoing, informal literacy assessment notebook.* Mansfield, OH: Ohio Department of Education.

Evans-Stout, K. (1998). Implications for collaborative instructional practice. In D. Pounder (Ed.), *Restructuring schools for collaboration: Promises and pitfalls* (pp. 121–134). Albany: State University of New York Press.

Fauske, J. R. (1999, November). *Conditions that sustain collaboration and encourage trust.* Paper presented at the meeting of the University Council of Educational Administration, Minneapolis, MN.

Fauske, J. R. (2002). Preparing school leaders: Understanding, experiencing, and implementing collaboration. *International Electronic Journal of Leadership in Learning, 6*(6). Retrieved February 4, 2005, from http://www.ucalgary.ca/~iejll/

Fauske, J. R., & Schelble, R. (2002, April). *Valuing teacher teams in school level reform.* Paper presented at the meeting of the American Educational Research Association, New Orleans, LA.

Fountas, I., & Pinnell, G. S. (1996). *Guided reading: Good first teaching for all children.* Portsmouth, NH: Heinemann.

Gagnon, J. G., & McLaughlin, M. J. (2004). Curriculum, assessment, and accountability in day treatment and residential schools. *Exceptional Children, 70*(3), 263–283.

Ganske, K. (2000). *Word journeys: Assessment-guided phonics, spelling, and vocabulary instruction.* New York: Guilford Press.

Garcia, E. (2002). *Student cultural diversity: Understanding and meeting the challenge.* Boston: Houghton Mifflin.

Gardner, H. (2000). *Intelligence reframed: Multiple intelligences for the 21st century.* New York: Basic Books.

Gardner, H. (1993). *Multiple intelligences: The theory in practice.* New York: Basic Books.

Glatthorn, A. A., Carr, J. F., & Harris, D. E. (1996). Planning and organizing for curriculum renewal. In *ASCD Curriculum Handbook.* Alexandria, VA: Association for Supervision and Curriculum Development.

Gober, S. (2002). *Six simple ways to assess young children.* New York: Delmar.

Goertz, M., & Duffy, M. (2003). Mapping the landscape of high-stakes testing and accountability programs. *Theory into Practice, 42*(1), 4–11.

Goleman, D. (1995). *Emotional intelligence: Why it can matter more than I.Q.* New York: Bantam.

Gonzalez, V., Brusca-Vega, R., & Yawkey, T. (1997). *Assessment and instruction of culturally and linguistically diverse students with or at-risk of learning problems: From research to practice.* Boston: Allyn & Bacon.

Goodman, Y., Watson, D., & Burke, C. (1987). *Reading miscue inventory: Alternative procedures.* Katonah, NY: Richard Irwin.

Gregory, G. H., & Chapman, C. (2002). *Differentiated instructional strategies: One size doesn't fit all.* Thousand Oaks, CA: Corwin.

Guskey, T. R. (2003). How classroom assessment improves learning. *Educational Leadership, 60*(5), 6–11.

Hambleton, R. K. (1996). Advances in assessment models, methods, and practices. In D. C. Berliner & R. C. Caffee (Eds.), *The handbook of educational psychology* (pp. 899–925). New York: Macmillan.

Hamerstrom, J., Rutenbeck, J., Menke, C., Dorman, C., Genkinger, C., McCandless, D., & Kelly, B. (2002). *Definition of diverse learners.* Retrieved April 18, 2005, from http://www.aea16.k12.ia.us/ProDev/DLCommitte.htm

Hammeken, P.A. (2000). *Inclusion: A practical guide for all educators who teach students with disabilities—450 strategies for success.* Minnetonka, MN: Peytral.

Harrington-Lueker, D. (1991). Beyond multiple choice tests: The push to assess performance. *The Executive Educator, 13*(4), 20–22.

Harvey, S., & Goudvis, A. (2000). *Strategies that work: Teaching comprehension to enhance understanding.* Portland, ME: Stenhouse.

Hasan, R. (1984). The nursery tale as genre. *Linguistic Circular, 13,* 71–102.

Haynes, J., & O'Loughlin, J. (1999a). Meeting the challenge of content instruction in the K–8 classroom: Part 1. *TESOL Matters, 9*(2). Retrieved December 8, 2005, from http://www.tesol.org/s_tesol/sec_document.asp?CID=196&DID=554

Haynes, J., & O'Loughlin, J. (1999b). Meeting the challenge of content instruction in the K–8 Classroom: Part 2. *TESOL Matters, 9*(3). Retrieved December 8, 2005, from http://www.tesol.org/s_tesol/sec_document.asp?CID=196&DID=566

Henderson, E. H. (1990). *Teaching spelling* (2nd ed.). Boston: Houghton Mifflin.

Herman, J. (1996). Technical quality matters. In R. E. Blum & J. A. Arter (Eds.), *A handbook for student performance assessment in an era of restructuring* (pp. 1–6). Alexandria, VA: Association for Supervision and Curriculum Development.

Hilliard, A. G., III. (2000). Excellence in education versus high-stakes standardized testing. *Journal of Teacher Education, 51*(4), 293–304.

Hord, S. (1997). *Professional learning communities: Communities of continuous inquiry and improvement.* Retrieved February 19, 2005, from http://www.sedl.org/pubs/change34/welcome.html

Hundt, T. A. (2002). Videotaping young children in the classroom. *Teaching Exceptional Children, 34*(3), 38–43.

Individuals with Disabilities Improvement Act of 2004, H.R. 1350. (2004).

Jacobs, J. S., & Tunnel, M. O. (2004). *Children's literature, briefly.* Upper Saddle River, NJ: Merrill.

Jensen, E. (1998). *Teaching with the brain in mind.* Alexandria, VA: Association for Supervision and Curriculum Development.

Jones, P., & Swain, J. (2001). Parents' perceptions of annual reviews. *British Journal of Special Education, 28*(2), 60–65.

Keene, E. O., & Zimmermann, S. (1997). *Mosaic of thought: Teaching comprehension in a reader's workshop.* Portsmouth, NH: Heinemann.

Kohn, A. (1993). *Punished by rewards: The trouble with gold stars, incentive plans, A's, praise, and other bribes.* Boston: Houghton Mifflin.

Kohn, A. (2000). Burnt at the high stakes. *Journal of Teacher Education, 51*(4), 315–327.

Krashen, S. D. (2003). *Explorations in language acquisition and use.* Portsmouth, NH: Heinemann.

Kubiszyn, T., & Borich, G. (2003). *Educational testing and measurement: Classroom application and practice* (7th ed.). New York: John Wiley & Sons.

Laing, S. P., & Kamhi, A. (2003). Alternative assessment of language and literacy in culturally and linguistically diverse populations. *Language, Speech, and Hearing Services in Schools, 34,* 44–55.

Lane, S. (2004). Validity of high stakes assessment: Are students engaged in complex thinking? *Educational Measurement: Issues and Practice, 23*(3), 6–14.

Larkin, E. (2000). Teacher research: An ethnography of changing practice. *Teaching and Change, 7*(4), 347–362.

Lim, L., & Colgan, L. (2005). Implementing multiple assessments in mathematics: An action research study of one teacher and his students. *The Ontario Action Researcher.* Retrieved November 28, 2005, from http://www.nipissingu.ca/oar/PDFS/V713.pdf

Linn, R. L., Baker, E. L., & Betebenner, D. W. (2002). Accountability systems: Implications of the requirements of the No Child Left Behind Act of 2001. *Educational Researcher, 31*(6), 3–16.

Lizotte, D. (1998). *Learning from experience: Action research. Adventures in Assessment, 11.* Retrieved November 28, 2005, from http://www.sabes.org/resources/adventures/vol11/11lizotte.htm

Louis, K. S., & Kruse, S. D. (1995). *Professionalism and community: Perspectives on reforming urban schools.* Thousand Oaks, CA: Corwin.

Major, R. C., Fitzmaurice, S. F., Bunta, F., & Balasubramanian, C. (2002). The effects of nonnative accents on listening comprehension: Implications for ESL assessment. *TESOL Quarterly, 36*(2), 173–190.

McClean, J. E. (1997). Teacher empowerment through action research. *Kappa Delta Pi Record, 34*(1), 34–38.

McConnell, S. R., & Odum, S. L. (1999). A multimeasure performance-based assessment of social competence in young children with disabilities. *Topics in Early Childhood Special Education, 9*(2), 67–76.

McKenzie, W. (1999). Multiple Intelligence Survey. Retrieved May 15, 2005, from http://surfaquarium.com/mi/inventory.htm

McMillan, J. H. (2001). *Essential assessment concepts for teachers and administrators.* Thousand Oaks, CA: Corwin.

McMillan, J. H. (2004). *Classroom assessment: Principles and practices for effective instruction* (3rd ed.). Boston: Allyn & Bacon.

McMillan, J.H., & Nash, S. (2000, April). Teacher classroom assessment and grading practices. Paper presented at the meeting of the National Council on Measurement in Education, New Orleans, LA.

McMunn, N., McColskey, W., & Butler, S. (2004). Building teacher capacity in classroom assessment to improve student learning. *International Journal of Educational Policy, Research, & Practice, 4*(4), 25–48. Retrieved December 1, 2005, from www.serve.org/_downloads/REL/Assessment/Built_Teacher%20Cap.pdf

McNair, S., Bhargava, A., Adams, L., Edgerton, S., & Kypros, B. (2003). Teachers speak out on assessment practices. *Early Childhood Education Journal, 31*(1), 23–31.

McTighe, J., & Ferrera, S. (1996). Performance-based assessment in the classroom: A planning framework. In R. E. Blum & J. A. Arter (Eds.), *A handbook for student performance assessment in an era of restructuring* (pp. 1–9). Alexandria, VA: Association for Supervision and Curriculum Development.

Mettetal, G. (2002–2003). Improving teaching through classroom action research. *Essays on teaching excellence: Toward the best in the academy, 14*(7). Retrieved November 29, 2005, from http://academic.udayton.edu/FacDev/Newsletters/EssaysforTeaching-Excellence/PODvol14/tevol14n7.html

Mindes, G., Ireton, H., & Mardell-Czudnowski, C. (1996). *Assessing young children.* Albany, NY: Delmar.

Morris, R. D. (1981). Concept of word: A developmental phenomenon in the beginning reading and writing processes. *Language Arts, 58,* 659–668.

Morrow, R. D. (1991). The challenge of Southeast Asian parental involvement. *Principal, 70*(3), 20–22.

National Commission on Excellence in Education. (1983). *A nation at risk.* Washington, DC: U.S. Department of Education. Retrieved October 3, 2005, from http://www.ed.gov/pubs/NatAtRisk/index.html

National Reading Panel. (2000). *Teaching children to read: An evidence-based assessment of the scientific research literature on reading and its implications for reading instruction.* Washington, DC: National Institute of Child Health and Human Development, National Institutes of Health.

Nitko, A. J. (2004). *Educational assessment of students* (4th ed.). Upper Saddle River, NJ: Pearson.

No Child Left Behind Act of 2001, Pub. L. No. 107–110. (2001).

O'Moore, L. (1997). *Inclusion: Strategies for working with young children.* Minnetonka, MN: Peytral.

Oswego City School District (n.d.). *Standards-based unit writing: Day 2.* Oswego, NY: Author.

Phye, G. D. (Ed.). (1997). *Handbook of classroom assessment: Learning, adjustment, and achievement.* San Diego, CA: Academic Press.

Popham, W. J. (2005). *Classroom assessment: What teachers need to know* (4th ed.). Boston: Allyn & Bacon.

Popham, W. J. (2003). *Test better, teach better: The instructional role of assessment.* Alexandria, VA: Association for Supervision and Curriculum Development.

Putnam, R. T., & Borko, H. (2000). What do new views of knowledge and thinking have to say about research on teacher learning? *Educational Researcher, 29,* 4–15.

Raywid, M. A. (1993). Finding time for collaboration. *Educational Leadership, 51*(1), 30–34.

Read, C. (1975). *Children's categorizations of speech sounds in English* (Vol. 17). Urbana, IL: National Council of Teachers of English.

Readence, J. E., Bean, T. W., & Baldwin, R. S. (1995). *Content area literacy: An integrated approach* (5th ed.). Dubuque, IA: Kendall/Hunt.

Reeves, D. (2004). *Accountability for learning: How teachers and school leaders can take charge.* Alexandria, VA: Association for Supervision and Curriculum Development.

Rodgers, C. (2002). Defining reflection: Another look at John Dewey and reflective thinking. *Teachers College Record, 104*(4), 842–866.

Rosenholtz, S. J. (1991). *Teachers' workplace: The social organization of schools.* New York: Teachers College Press.

Rushton, S. (2001). Applying brain research to create developmentally appropriate learning environments. *Young Children, 56*, 76–82.

Rushton, S., Eitelgeorge, J., & Zickafoose, R. (2003). Connecting Cambourne's conditions of learning to brain-mind principles: Application for the classroom teacher. *Early Childhood Education Journal 31*, 11–21.

Sagor, R. (2005). *The action research guidebook.* Thousand Oaks, CA: Corwin.

Schmoker, M. (2003). First thing first: Demystifying data analysis. *Educational Leadership, 60*(5), 22–24.

Schön, D. A. (1983). *The reflective practitioner.* New York: Basic Books.

Schön, D. A. (1987). *Educating the reflective practitioner.* San Francisco: Jossey-Bass.

Sergiovanni, T. J. (1994). *Building communities in schools.* San Francisco: Jossey-Bass.

Sheinker, J., & Redfield, D. (2001) *Handbook for professional development in assessment literacy.* Washington, DC: Council of Chief State School Officers.

Shrum, J, & Glisan, E. (2004). *Teacher's handbook: Contextualized language instruction* (3rd ed.). Boston: Heinle & Heinle.

Smith, M. L., & Fey, P. (2000). Validity and accountability in high-stakes testing. *Journal of Teacher Education, 51*(5), 334–344.

Stiggins, R. (1997). *Student-centered classroom assessment* (2nd ed.). Upper Saddle River, NJ: Merrill.

Stiggins, R. J. (2005). *Student-involved assessment for learning* (4th ed.). Upper Saddle River, NJ: Pearson.

Sylwester, R. (1997). The neurobiology of self-esteem and aggression. *Educational Leadership, 54*(5), 75–79.

Teele, S. (1997). *Teele inventory of multiple intelligences.* Redlands, CA: Sue Teele & Associates.

Tilton, L. (2000). *Inclusion: A fresh look—Practical strategies to help all students succeed.* Shorewood, MN: Covington Cove.

Tomlinson, C. A. (2001). *How to differentiate instruction in mixed ability classrooms* (2nd ed.). Alexandria, VA: Association for Supervision and Curriculum Development.

Trepanier-Street, M. (2001). *The views of teachers on assessment: A comparison of lower and upper elementary teachers.* Retrieved June 9, 2005, from http://www.soe.umd.umich.edu/soe/UMD_SOE_PR_2001/ViewsofTeachersonAssessment.pdf

Trepanier-Street, M. L., McNair, S., & Donegan, M. M. (2001). The views of teachers on assessment. *Journal of Research in Childhood Education, 15*(20), 234–241.

Triandis, H. C. (1996). The psychological measurement of cultural syndromes. *American Psychologist, 51*, 407–415.

Trice, A. D. (2000). *A handbook of classroom assessment.* New York: Longman.

U.S. Census Bureau. (2004). Census 2000. Retrieved December 7, 2005, from http://www.census.gov//population/www/socdemo/lang_use.html

Vermont Department of Education and Vermont Institute for Science, Mathematics, and Technology. (2002). *Leadership advisory #1: Technical considerations at four levels: Tools and resources for local comprehensive assessment systems.* Montpelier, VT: Vermont Department of Education. Retrieved August 16, 2005, from http://www.vermontinstitutes.org/assessment/clas/leadershipadv1.pdf

Villa, R. A., & Thousand, J. (Eds). (2005). *Creating an inclusive school* (2nd ed.). Alexandria, VA: Association for Supervision and Curriculum Development.

Vygotsky, L. S. (1978). *Mind in society: The development of higher psychological processes.* Cambridge, MA: Harvard University Press.

Wade, S., & Fauske, J. (2004). Dialogue online: Prospective teachers' discourse strategies in computer mediated discussions. *Reading Research Quarterly, 29*(2), 134–159.

Waite-Stupiansky, S. (1997). *Building understanding together: A constructivist approach to early childhood education.* New York: Delmar.

Wenning, R., Herdman, P. A., Smith, N., McMahon, N., & Washington, K. (2003). *No Child Left Behind: Testing, reporting, and accountability.* Retrieved October 3, 2005, from http://www.ericdigests.org/2004–2/behind.html

Wilson, G. P., Martens, P., & Arya, P. (2005). Accountability for reading and readers: What the numbers don't tell. *The Reading Teacher, 58*(7), 622–631.

Wilson, M., & Sloane, K. (2000). From principles to practice: An embedded assessment system. *Applied Measurement in Education, 13*(2), 181–208.

Wolfendale, S. (2004). *Getting the balance right: Towards partnership in assessing children's developmental and educational achievement.* Retrieved June 9, 2005, from http://www.teachernet.gov.uk/docbank/index.cfm?id=7302

Yopp, H. K. (1995). Yopp-Singer test of phoneme segmentation. *The Reading Teacher, 49*(1), 22.

Zutell, J., & Rasinski, T. V. (1991). Training teachers to attend to their students' oral fluency. *Theory into Practice, 30*(3), 211–217.

About the Editors and Contributors

Rosemarie L. Ataya is an assessment specialist with the Department of Defense Education Activity (DoDEA). Dr. Ataya's research is concentrated in the area of instrument and rubric development and validation. She has published her research in journals such as *Educational and Psychological Measurement* and *Instructional Science*. At the University of South Florida, Dr. Ataya was an Assistant Professor in the Department of Educational Measurement and Research. She taught courses in measurement, research methods, and program evaluation on both the graduate and undergraduate levels. Prior to obtaining her doctorate, she served as a middle school social studies teacher for 7 years in Massachusetts.

Judy F. Carr has been a middle grades language arts teacher, a school district administrator, a college professor, and a project director for several statewide initiatives in Vermont. Currently she is senior lecturer in the Department of Educational Leadership and Policy Studies at the University of South Florida Sarasota-Manatee. She is also Co-Director of the Center for Curriculum Renewal, which supports systems development, leadership development, and the design of curriculum and assessment in school districts in Florida, Vermont, New York, and South Carolina. She is coauthor of *Creating Dynamic Schools Through Mentoring, Coaching, and Collaboration* (ASCD, 2005); *How to Use Standards in the Classroom* (ASCD, 1996); *Getting It Together: A Process Workbook for K–12 Curriculum Development, Implementation, and Assessment* (Allyn & Bacon, 1992); and *Succeeding with Standards* (ASCD, 2001). She is coeditor of *Living and Learning in the Middle Grades: The Dance Continues; A Festschrift for Chris Stevenson* (National Middle School Association, 2001) and *Integrated Studies in the Middle Grades: Dancing Through Walls* (Teachers College Press, 1993).

Janice Eitelgeorge began her teaching career as a high school choral director and an elementary music teacher. She received her M.A. and Ph.D. from the Ohio State University. She has taught at the Ohio State University, Ohio Wesleyan University, Mt. Vernon Nazarene College, and Otterbein College. At the University of South Florida, she taught master's-level courses in literacy research and pedagogy. Her research interests focus on literacy assessment and writing development.

Janice Fauske began her career as a 7th-grade English teacher in a rural, economically deprived school district in Virginia. After earning an M.S.Ed. in Reading Psychology, she taught special education in an inner-city school district and later moved to college teaching at a small Virginia college. She earned an Educational Specialist degree in Higher Education at the College of William and Mary and later completed her Ph.D. in Educational Administration at the University of Utah. Before joining the faculty at the University of South Florida as Associate Professor in Educational Leadership and Policy Studies, Dr. Fauske worked as the Assistant Commissioner for Academic Affairs at the Utah State Board of Regents, as a faculty member and administrator at Weber State University, as founding Dean of the School of Education at Westminster College, and Associate Professor and Doctoral Advisor in Educational Leadership and Policy at the University of Utah.

Stephen Graves's professional experiences include teaching undergraduate and graduate students at the University of South Florida; the University of Memphis; the University of Alabama at Birmingham; the University of South Carolina; Coastal Carolina University; and Manchester College in Oxford, England. He has taught 3-year-olds, 5-year-olds in public school kindergarten, and child development students at two 2-year colleges in South Carolina. Dr. Graves was the Senior Editor of the *International Journal of Early Childhood* from 2000 to 2003. He is Past President of the National Organization of Child Development Laboratory Schools, the Alabama Association of Young Children, and the South Carolina Association on Children Under Six. He is coauthor of *Empowering At-Risk Families During the Early Childhood Years* (National Education Association, 1993) and *Young Children: An Introduction to Early Childhood Education* (West, 1996).

Phyllis Jones is an Assistant Professor in the Department of Special Education at the University of South Florida Sarasota-Manatee. Upon earning her bachelor's degree in the education of children with severe learning disabilities, Phyllis taught and was an administrator for 15 years in schools in the United Kingdom. Her master's in Special Education is from Durham University, the United Kingdom. While completing her doctoral work, she was a faculty member for 5 years in the College of Education at Northumbria University, also in the United Kingdom. Her Ph.D. research relates to teacher thinking about pupils with profound and multiple learning disabilities. Phyllis is an international scholar at the Universities Council for the Education of Teachers/American Association of Colleges for Teacher Education (UCET/ACCTE), having received funding to research teacher education programs in special education on the East and West Coasts in the United States. Phyllis is coinvestigator of an Economic and Social and Research Council (United Kingdom) project that focuses upon engaging disabled people in the discourse of inclusion. She is author of *Inclusion in the Early Years: Stories of Good Practice* (David Fulton, 2005) and is published widely in international journals related to inclusion, special education, and teacher education. She is a reviewer for the *British Journal of Special Education* and on the Research Advisory Board for Sunfield Center, in the United Kingdom. She is on the advisory board for the Florida Inclusion Network, a board member of the Sunset Chapter of the Council for Exceptional Children, a committee member of the International Inclusion Committee of the Association for Persons with Special Handicaps, and also a steering and advisory board member for the University of South Florida Professional Development Preparation Grant. She is also a subcontractor, working collaboratively with the University of Florida and Florida State University, on the Florida Developmental Disabilities grant project, Florida Low Incidence Personnel Preparation Project. Phyllis is a recipient of the Outstanding Undergraduate Teaching Award (2004–2005) at the University of South Florida.

Anne Marie Juola-Rushton teaches at Virgil Mills Elementary in Palmetto, Florida, where she is presently teaching 3rd grade after looping with her students from last year. Anne was a preschool director in Michigan for 9 years and is now completing her Ph.D. in Early Childhood Education at the University of South Florida.

Sharon Miller Keller works in assessment with the Ohio Department of Education. She was formerly an Assistant Professor at the University of South Florida. She began her teaching career as an elementary classroom teacher. Early on, she was involved in curricular reform in the areas of professional teacher development, literacy, and assessment reform through the projects of Classrooms of Future, the Primary Learning Assessment System, and Literacy Institutes in Ohio. Later she taught language arts and reading methods, curriculum foundations and curriculum design, and qualitative research methods and action research for classroom teachers at Bowling Green State University. Her research interests include literacy and at-risk learners, as well as professional development in teacher education.

Karen Kent received her B.S. in Education and M.A. in Literacy Education from the Ohio State University. She was an elementary classroom teacher for 15 years and later served as a Literacy Education Consultant for 18 Ohio school districts at the Mid-Ohio Educational Resource Center. In this position, she conducted literacy assessment and instruction workshops for classroom teachers, as well as writing literacy grants for the school districts.

Elizabeth Larkin is an Associate Professor in the College of Education and teaches courses in the Early Childhood and Elementary Teacher Certification Programs. Prior to coming to the University of South Florida in 1998, Dr. Larkin taught for 12 years at Wheelock College in Boston, where she was a tenured faculty member of the Graduate School and worked as a liaison in a Professional Development School collaboration. She has also taught in the primary grades and been the director of a preschool and day care. Her research interests include looking at the professional development of educators, as well as studying intergenerational initiatives that bring older adults and younger populations together for their mutual benefit. She is the author of "Teacher Research: An Ethnography of Changing Practice" (*Teaching & Change,* 7[4], 2000). She is on the editorial board of the *Journal of Intergenerational Relationships.*

Weimin Mo was born in Shanghai, China and is currently an Associate Professor in the College of Education at the University of South Florida. He received his B.A. from Shanghai Institute of Foreign Languages and taught English as a second language in China for 15 years before he came to this country to further his study. He got both his M.Ed. and Ed.D. from Indiana University of Pennsylvania. He was an elementary school teacher in Pennsylvania for 3 years and has been in higher education for 10 years. His research interests are children's literature, literacy learning, and multicultural education. He is currently on the editorial board of the National Council of Teachers of English's journal *Language Arts* and is a reviewer for the international journal *Children's Literature in Education.*

Stephen Rushton supervises student teachers and teaches courses in research, elementary education methods, and the writing process. He is presently working with two Professional Development Schools in Sarasota County while working with master's of education students. Dr. Rushton previously taught elementary education for 12 years in Ontario, Canada, and Oak Ridge, Tennessee. He is conducting research on teacher effectiveness, brain-based teaching approaches, and personality types using the Myers-Briggs Inventory. Dr. Rushton was recently awarded the Outstanding Undergraduate Teaching Award (2001) by his peers at University of South Florida at Sarasota-Manatee and the Outstanding Professor Award by the 2003 graduating class.

Susan Sheffield is currently Director of Teacher Education at Manatee Community College and is an Adjunct Instructor in the College of Education at the University of South Florida. She teaches undergraduate and graduate courses in special education. Her research interests involve teacher training, the use of evidenced-based teaching methods in special education classrooms, and alternative teacher-training programs. She earned her B.A. in Liberal Arts English from the State University of New York at Plattsburgh, and her M.A. in Varying Exceptionalities and Ph.D. in Curriculum and Instruction from the University of South Florida at Tampa. She began her teaching career in the Los Angeles Unified School District teaching at-risk urban minority students. Upon moving to Tampa, she taught at the Vanguard School, an international residential school for students with learning disabilities in Lake Wales, Florida. While a doctoral student at University of South Florida at Tampa, she coordinated two federal grant programs involving an accelerated graduate program and a program designed to help paraprofessionals earn teaching degrees and certification in special education. Before coming to the Sarasota/Manatee campus from the Florida Mental Health Institute/University of South Florida, she coordinated a 4-year federal grant titled "Whole School Reform: Creating Environments that Work for All Children" that focused on collaborating with special education classroom teachers to identify and implement research-based teaching strategies in the areas of reading, formative assessment, positive behavior support, and parent/family involvement.

G. Pat Wilson is an Assistant Professor of Childhood Education at the University of South Florida, Sarasota-Manatee. Her sister Kathy inspired her to become a special education teacher wherein she taught in institutional, private, and public school settings. She has held administrative roles, highlighted by directing the special services programs for a school district in Maine. With a long interest in how children learn to read, she became a reading specialist and earned her doctorate in Reading and Writing Instruction from the University of New Hampshire. She has coauthored several articles and chapters that focused on the impact of reading instruction programs on children's strategy use, including: "An Inquiry into Children's Reading in One Urban School Using SRA Reading Mastery" (*Journal of Literacy Research*, in press); "Influences on Retellings: Learning from High and Low Retellers," in Y. Goodman & P. Martens, (Eds.), *Critical Issues in Early Literacy Development: Research and Pedagogy* (Lawrence Erlbaum Associates, in press); "Reclaiming Literacy Instruction: Evidence in Support of Literature-Based Programs" (*Language Arts, 83*[1], 2005); "Accountability for Reading and Readers: What the Numbers Don't Tell" (*The Reading Teacher, 58*[7], 2005); "The Impact of Reading Mastery on Children's Learning," in B. Altwerger (Ed.), *Reading for Profit: How the Bottom Line Leaves Kids Behind* (Heinemann, 2005); and "Readers, Instruction, and the NRP" (*Kappan, 86*[3], 2004).

 **Index**